The Audacious Revolution

The Audacious Revolution

10 Steps to Being Audacious for God

Glyn Barrett

New Wine Press

New Wine Ministries
PO Box 17
Chichester
West Sussex
United Kingdom
PO20 6YB

ISBN 1-903725-44-5

Typeset by CRB Associates, Reepham, Norfolk
Cover design by CCD, www.ccdgroup.co.uk
Printed in the United States of America

Contents

Dedication

To Dave and Jen, you are "Revolutionaries!" You are everything Audacious Revolutionaries should be – bold, fearless, daring, dangerous, cheeky, unrestrained by convention, spirited, original and free. What else can I say about you? You are amazing!

To all the Audacious Revolutionary forerunners; Jesus, Tertullian, Luther, Latimer, Ridley, Gilpin, Wesley, Spurgeon, Dad. Thanks for setting us up for victory!

To the current generation of Audacious Revolutionaries: Let's do God proud!

Acknowledgements

To my family: Sophia, Georgia and Jaedon. Life is great with you! You amaze me every day. Also Mum and Sian, thanks for being you!

To my editor, Gill. Thanks for correcting my syntax, grammar, spelling, and punctuation! Who would have thought someone with an accent like yours could do such an amazing job editing a book! Great job!

To my friends: Stuart, Mark and Derek – thanks for friendship, fun and curry.

To my church and network: Hope City Church, Youth Alive UK and Audacious. You are all great people. I look at you and realise, "We can do it!"

To my mentors: Dave, Mal, and Russ; you set the pace!

To Andy Hawthorne: You are a great Revolutionary!

To my publisher, Tim. Thanks for your patience, commitment and resonance.

To my Revolutionary team: Foz and Em, Laney, Naomi, Lindsey (with an e), Andy and Karen, Karly, Dee, Phil, Steve and Shuv, the Band (great album! – Jen your voice rocks!), the two with freckles, Chris and Gosia (and Levi?!), Reidy, Mrs Waddams, Michael, Nick and Caz, Nate and Nikki, thanks for life!

To my God and THE ULTIMATE REVOLUTONARY – JESUS CHRIST! I live to honour you!

A Revolutionary Speaks!

What a thrill it's been to read this book! Is there any message that needs to be heard louder than this one? Young people who are filled with the Spirit of Jesus and living His revolutionary gospel out, have always and will always change the world for the better.

I love the first words of the book of Acts where Luke, who has finished writing his story of the life, death, resurrection and ascension of Jesus and now wants to get on with telling the story of the Church that was born on the back of all that went on, says, *"In my former book, Theophilus, I wrote about all that Jesus* ***began*** *to do and to teach . . . "* That's right, the gospel of Luke was just the beginning. Jesus wants right now, at the start of the 21st Century, to continue teaching and doing stuff through ordinary, audacious, revolutionaries like you and me. He really does want us, by the power of His Spirit within, to do the stuff in our situations that turned the world upside down 2,000 years ago.

If only one or two of you who are going to read these pages get it – I mean *really* get it – the implications for this generation will be massive.

So read on, but whatever you do, don't just agree with what Glyn has got to say. Get hold of it, let it sink in and then ... join the revolution!

Andy Hawthorne
CEO of The Message Trust
www.message.org.uk

Understanding the Terms

1. Audacious

au·da·cious: (ô-dā'shəs)
[***French*** *audacieux, from* **Old French** *audace, boldness, from* **Latin** *audācia, from audāx, audāc-, bold, from audēre, to dare, from avidus, avid.*]

Meaning:

- ***bold***
- ***fearless***
- ***cheeky***
- ***daring***
- ***dangerous***
- ***unrestrained by convention***
- ***spirited***
- ***original***

(i) ***Invulnerable to fear or intimidation***; adj. "audacious explorers"; "fearless adventurers"; "intrepid pioneers" [syn.: brave, dauntless, fearless, intrepid, unfearing]

(ii) ***Unrestrained by convention or propriety***; "an audacious trick to pull"; [syn.: barefaced, bodacious, bold-faced, brassy, brazen, brazen-faced, insolent]

(iii) ***Predisposed to venture or take risks***; "audacious visions of the total conquest of space"; "the most daring of a venturous spirit" [syn.: daring, venturesome, venturous]

2. Revolution

rev·o·lu·tion: (rĕv'ə-lo͞o'shən)
[***Middle English*** *revolucioun, from Old French revolution, from Late* ***Latin*** *revolūti, revolūtiōn-, from* ***Latin*** *revolūtus, past participle of revolvere, to turn over.*]

Meaning:

- ***overthrow one government and replace with another***
- ***a sudden or momentous change in a situation***

(i) ***A drastic and far-reaching change in ways of thinking and behaving***; n. "the industrial revolution was also a cultural revolution"

(ii) ***The overthrow of a government*** by those who are governed.

3. Revolutionary

rev·o·lu·tion·ar·y: (rĕv'ə-lo͞o'shə-nĕr'ē)

Meaning:

- ***one who takes part in a revolution!***

(i) ***Introducing radical change***; adj. "a revolutionary discovery"; "radical political views" [syn.: radical]

(ii) ***Relating to or having the nature of a revolution***; "revolutionary wars"; "the Revolutionary era"

(iii) ***Advocating or engaged in revolution***; "revolutionary pamphlets"; "a revolutionary junta" [ant.: counter-revolutionary] n. a radical supporter of political or social revolution [syn.: revolutionist]

A Note from the Author

Careful! This is a dangerous book! Reading the pages of *The Audacious Revolution* is likely to stir up the trouble-causing, cheeky, daring, dangerous, bold, spirited person within you. Jesus was exactly that! He was all of those qualities and more! If you thought Jesus was boring, you were wrong! If you thought He was a dangerous revolutionary, you were absolutely right!

The Audacious Revolution is written for young people who are seeking to rise up and live out the words of the apostle Paul written nearly 2,000 years ago:

> *"I am not ashamed of the gospel, because it is the power of God for the salvation of everyone who believes . . ."*
>
> (Romans 1:16)

This book is a companion to THE BOOK – THE BIBLE. You need your Bible with you as you read *The Audacious Revolution.*

Join the revolution!

Glyn Barrett

Four (and more) Audacious Revolutionaries

When King Henry the Eighth of England died, his son Edward became the new king. Under his kingship, church services which were previously in Latin, were translated into English so "English people" could understand what was going on in church! This was just one of his many radical reforms.

When Edward died his sister Mary became Queen. She was determined to change the church back to the "old way" of doing things. Had she shown a little more diplomacy she might have succeeded, but she was opinionated and headstrong, and would take no advice from her advisors. As Mary's mother had been Spanish, she was determined to marry the heir to Spain's throne, not realizing how much the English feared that this would make their country a province of the Spanish Empire.

Mary insisted that the best way to deal with heresy (changing church from Latin to English plus moving from "priest centred" Catholicism to "people centred" Protestantism) was to burn heretics. During her five-year reign as queen, she burnt nearly three hundred "Religious Revolutionaries" at the stake, the most famous of which were the "Oxford Martyrs".

Hugh Latimer was a famous preacher. He was the

Bishop of Worcester during King Henry's reign, but resigned when the king refused to allow the new church reforms (Protestantism) that Latimer desired. When Mary became queen, he was arrested and tried for heresy. After being found guilty, he was burnt at the stake, along with his friend Nicholas Ridley. His final words have rung through history:

> **"Be of good cheer, Master Ridley, and play the man, for we shall this day light such a candle in England as I trust by God's grace shall never be put out."**

His friend Nicholas Ridley was the private chaplain to both Archbishop Thomas Cranmer and King Henry. While Edward was king, Ridley was part of the team that created the first "English Book of Common Prayer". When Mary came to the throne, he was arrested, tried, and burnt with Latimer in Oxford on 16 October 1555.

Archbishop Thomas Cranmer was the "mover and shaker" when it came to translating common worship practices into English and establishing new forms of worship in church. When Mary became queen, Cranmer was caught between wanting to honour the queen (because it was godly to do so) and following the convictions of his heart, which meant opposing the queen's stance on priest verses people-centred church life. Queen Mary ordered Cranmer to return to the old way of church and swear allegiance to the Pope in Rome. On five separate occasions, Cranmer wrote a letter of submission to the Pope, and four times he tore it up before sending it. Eventually, however, he wrote the letter and submitted it. Queen Mary wasn't sure of Cranmer's sincerity and so she ordered him to be burned at the stake in Oxford on 21 March 1556.

Just before he died, he renounced his letter of submission and declared that he died not as a follower of the "old tradition", but the new, fresh, vibrant way of doing church and Christianity. He said, "I have sinned, in that I signed with my hand what I did not believe with my heart. When the flames are lit, this hand shall be the first to burn." When the fire was lit, he leaned forward and held his right hand in the flames. The only other movement he made on the pyre that day was to wipe the sweat from his forehead.

Radiating from the same pages of history comes another revolutionary – Bernard Gilpin. His catch-phrase was the scripture, *"All things work together for the good of those who love Him . . . "* (Romans 8:28).

Queen Mary's officers seized Gilpin to burn him at the stake. On the road to London, he was treated so badly that he broke his leg. All the soldiers gathered around and said, "All things work together for good, do they?" Because of the ordeal, he was delayed a day or so on his travels to the tower of London. He arrived just in time to hear that Elizabeth had been proclaimed queen and that Mary was now under lock and key herself. He had escaped death! He said to the soldiers around him, "I told you. Now do you believe me, that all things work together for good?" Bernard Gilpin became known as "the apostle of the North", bringing the message of salvation and grace to the cities and villages in the north of England.

Revolutionaries have gone before us. It is because of them that we have all that we have today! When these four revolutionaries lived, the church in Britain was in desperate need of a revolution!

Church history is full of Revolutionaries:

- In the second century AD, Tertullian said "I am safe, if I am not ashamed of my Lord ... the Son of God was crucified; I am not ashamed because others are ashamed of it. And the Son of God died; it is definitely to be believed, because it is foolish. He was buried and rose again; it is certain because it is impossible!"[1] When he spoke these words, the world was in need of a revolution!

- In 1519, Martin Luther said about Romans 1:17, "I meditated night and day on those words until at last, by the mercy of God I noticed their context: 'The righteousness of God is revealed in it, as it is written: "The righteous person lives by faith."' I began to understand that in this verse the 'righteousness of God' means the way in which a righteous person lives through a gift of God – that is, *by faith*. I began to understand that this verse means that the righteousness of God is revealed through the Gospel, but it is a *passive* righteousness, that is, it is by the merciful God which makes us righteous by faith ... all at once I felt like I had been born again and entered into paradise itself through open gates. Immediately I saw the whole of scripture in a different light."[2] When Luther said those words, the world was in desperate need of a revolution, and he started it!

- In the 1800s, Charles Haddon Spurgeon said, "A vigorous faith will often shut its eyes to difficulties; it laughs at impossibilities and cries 'It shall be done.' "[3] When he preached those words in Westminster tabernacle in London, Britain was in desperate need of a revolution!

Have you ever read words like that from the history books and thought, "I wish I had said that!": "Be of good cheer ... and play the man, for we shall this day light such a candle in England as I trust by God's grace shall never be put out." As a classic "statement motto" it created a revolution on a global scale!

Notes

1. Tertullian, *On the Flesh of Christ*, 5.4.
2. Jonathon Hill, *The History of Christian Thought*, Lion Publishing Plc, p. 178.
3. C.H. Spurgeon – "The Prince of Preachers".

The Audacious Revolution!

These men were used by God to start revolutions that were to have a world-wide impact. They weren't bloodthirsty revolutions that inflicted pain and suffering on the masses. They were revolutions in thinking and lifestyle that led many hundreds of thousands of people into relationship with Jesus Christ! Their lives had a dramatic effect on all major social institutions. Families were more inclined to stay together, hospitals and charities were formed, schools and universities were opened, laws protecting the rights of common people were passed, and the church had a massive impact in politics, education and the media.

Today, we live in an age where laws are made at government level which pay no attention to God's Word. The media portrays Jesus as some insipid fairy who sounds more like a child than the dangerous revolutionary He is, and in our schools and universities God is relegated to the back seat – if there is room for Him at all!

But there is good news! There is a rising generation of young people who are,

- ***Bold***
- ***Fearless***

- ***Cheeky***
- ***Daring***
- ***Dangerous***
- ***Unrestrained by convention***
- ***Spirited and***
- ***Original***

They are part of the AUDACIOUS REVOLUTION.

The Audacious Revolution is not a new revolution! It's the same revolution that started when Jesus came to earth 2,000 years ago. It's the same revolution that Tertullian, Luther, Latimer and Spurgeon lived so passionately for. Although it's been repackaged and re-branded for today, the passion and the message are the same. The conviction that compelled Latimer to walk to the stake and not recant his beliefs is rising in young people today.

There is a generation of young people who have had enough of,

- Mediocrity and half-heartedness
- Apologising for believing in "One Way" – Jesus Christ
- Powerless sermons, and
- Ineffective churches!

There are "Audacious Revolutionaries" who are determined to,

- Live "full-on for God"
- Show the world that living for Jesus is brilliant
- Change their world!

In Acts 5:12–29 we read about the Revolution that Jesus passed on to the disciples and from them, to us. There are five characteristics of the revolution that are important for you to understand if you too are going to be a Revolutionary.

1. It's a Power Revolution

If you were God, you probably wouldn't have chosen Peter to be on your team. So often he spoke or acted first and thought later. He could probably be described as being an "Oops!" kind of guy.

- "I'm going to walk on water ... Oops" (Matthew 14:22–36).
- "I'll follow you anywhere, Jesus ... Oops" (Luke 22:33–34, 54–62).
- "You'll never die, Jesus ... Oops" (Matthew 16:22–23).

Peter had a habit of saying the wrong thing at the wrong time – but something changed!

In Acts 1:8, we read; *"But you will receive power when the Holy Spirit comes on you ... "* That power transformed Peter.

In the animated movie, *The Incredibles*, Mr Incredible's arch-enemy, Syndrome started off as Mr Incredible's greatest fan. "Buddy", as he was known as a child, was not "a Super" (someone with extraordinary powers), yet he desperately wanted to be.

He made rocket boots and designed a "super-outfit" complete with cape (which ultimately contributed to his down-fall). Buddy didn't want to be ordinary. He wanted to be SUPER.

In Acts 1:8, God put His "Super" on Peter's "natural" and he was transformed into a supernatural man. The Audacious Revolution is a "Power Revolution". It's all about God's power (or "Super") on our natural minds, bodies and resources, enabling us to accomplish supernatural things. Naturally you may face a lot of obstacles in school, university and work. You may face difficulties with your health or face major issues because of your past. But when God's Power comes upon you, He gives you supernatural ways to overcome the biggest of natural problems.

You stop being natural and move into supernatural territory. The equation looks like this:

Your NATURAL + God's SUPER
= A SUPERNATURAL person and situation

In other words, anything is possible. The next time you think something is too difficult or impossible – STOP BEING NATURAL – You are a SUPER!

2. It's a Growing Revolution

In Acts 5:14 we read: "*Nevertheless, more and more men and women believed in the Lord and were added to their number . . .*"

In Matthew 16:18, Jesus says, *"I will build my church!"* At no point in the Bible do we read that Jesus goes on vacation or has a "bad hair day". God is totally committed to the growth of the revolution, to more and more people believing in, and living for Him. It's a "Growing Revolution".

In 1919, Edmund Hillary was born. He went to Auckland Grammar School in New Zealand. In the four hours that it took him to travel there and back from Tuakau each day, he filled his time by reading. He was younger and smaller than most of his class, lacking confidence in social settings. He also felt incompetent, awkward and uncoordinated at sport and so he took refuge in reading, and dreamed of a life filled with adventure. At sixteen, his interest in mountaineering began. He discovered that, while he was not a natural athlete, his gangly, taut frame was physically strong and had higher levels of endurance than many of his walking friends.

Hillary served in the New Zealand Air Force (WWII) for two years, as a navigator, but was discharged after an accident. By then he knew his ultimate dream: "Some day I'll climb Everest" he told a friend just before the war. He was certain, although no one believed him then. After being discharged from the Air Force he joined the Auckland division of the New Zealand Alpine Club.

After the war, Hillary spent much time preparing for Everest. He climbed in summer and winter to practise both rock climbing and ice-pick work, and also took up wrestling. In 1951 Hillary made his first trip to the Himalayas, and the following year joined a British

Everest Committee training team. In an interview he said,

> "We didn't know if it was humanly possible to reach the top of Mount Everest. And even using oxygen as we were, if we did get to the top, we weren't at all sure whether we wouldn't drop dead or something of that nature . . ."

Everest is 29,028 feet high. A mountain that was unreachable, fearless, deadly, and mysterious. Fifteen previous expeditions had been defeated in their attempts to conquer it. Many climbers had died on its slopes.

Hillary joined a British expedition of 400 climbers facing Everest in May, 1953. It was led by British mountaineer John Hunt who was keen to keep the expedition ahead of the monsoon snows. Climbers would be specifically selected to make the assault on Everest. One of the first pairs to attempt Everest had had to retire 300 feet short of the summit, so, being the strongest and fittest in the team, Hillary and a Nepalese Sherpa, Tenzing Norgay, were chosen to try the ascent.

After an uncomfortable night, they left the last camp at South Col in the freezing chill dawn of 29 May 1953. Five hours later, at 11:30am, Hillary, who was leading the climb at this point, stepped onto the summit. Hillary said, " . . . I then realised that the ridge ahead, instead of still monotonously rising, now dropped sharply away, and far below I could see the North Col and the Rongbuk Glacier. I looked upwards to see a narrow snow ridge running up to a snowy summit. A few more whacks of the ice-axe in the firm snow, and we stood on the top."

Sir Edmund Hillary had failed in several of his early attempts to climb Mount Everest. On one occasion, he had to leave five associates dead on the side of that great mountain. After one such unsuccessful attempt, in a meeting of mountaineers, he pointed to a photograph of Mount Everest and said, "I shall conquer you, for you have stopped growing, but I have not!"

What amazing determination from a brave adventurer, and what wise words: *"I shall conquer you, for you have stopped growing, but I have not."*

Obstacles may come between you and your God-given destiny, but the reality is that you have not stopped growing as a young man or woman of God. The moment you decide something is impossible or too difficult, you have put a ceiling on your life; you have limited your capabilities. The Revolution is growing, but so are you! Next time you hit an obstacle, change your focus and consider it an opportunity to become a bigger person.

Every day around the world, approximately 195,000 people become Christians.[4] If that statistic stays stable, in the next ten years over 7 billion people will give their lives to Christ. The point is simple ... it's a growing revolution!

3. It's an Unstoppable Revolution

Take a moment to read Acts 5:18–28 again. Also read verses 40–42. It's amazing that despite having been arrested, told not to preach about Jesus (see Acts 4:18–22), and threatened with further punishment, the apostles kept telling people the great news about Jesus.

Their mentality was simple: Devil you can;

- Beat us up – but you can't shut us up
- Knock us down – but you can't keep us down
- Lock us up – but you can't keep us out
- Stone us – but you won't defeat us
- Whip us – but you'll never stop this revolution!

... It'll pass from generation to generation, down through the ages until young people living in the "post-9/11 generation" get it and they will RISE with the revolution of Jesus Christ!

Acts 4:19 says powerfully. *"Judge for yourselves whether it is right in God's sight to obey you* [man's ideals] *rather than God!"*

- ▸ Society will try to shut you up and keep you down – but what is right?

- ▸ Society will attempt to fit you into a religious box – but what is right?

Throughout 2,000 years of the history of the church, governments and institutions have tried to stop the revolution!

- In China and Russia they banned the church and the Bible – but today in both of those countries the church continues to grow in huge numbers.

- Karl Marx, the founder of Communism famously said, "God is dead and we have killed him." Later he went insane and died – but God and the church lives on.

- Oasis famously said "We are bigger than God." While their albums don't sell so well any more, the Bible still tops the best seller list world-wide.

The point is simple – It's impossible to stop an "Unstoppable Revolution".

4. It's a Jesus Revolution

"Day after day, in the temple courts and from house to house, they never stopped teaching the good news that Jesus is the Christ!"

(Acts 5:42)

Some leaders want encounters with great leaders. Others want to have encounters at great conferences. Some want to read great books and teaching resources, and others still want to have encounters with famous celebrities. But it is meeting with Jesus that is the most amazing encounter you could ever have.

In Acts 4:13 it says:

> *"When they* [the rulers of the people] *saw the courage of Peter and John and realised that they were unschooled, ordinary men, they were astonished and took note that these men had been with Jesus."*

Something amazing happens when you spend time with Jesus!

In his book *The Glory of the Christ*, Peter Lewis shares a story. There was a young boy who had a hero who was famous for playing both football for the nation and cricket to county standard. His bedroom was a shrine, with every available space on the wall covered in posters of the great man. Once, while on holiday, the boy happened to meet his hero, and was invited to go fishing with him every morning. As the days rolled by and he spent more and more time with his hero, he realised that he wasn't perfect after all; he had bad breath in the morning, he had sleep in his eyes and bed-hair. In fact he says, "The more I got to know my hero, the smaller he became, because I realised he was just a normal man. But as I got older, I found a new hero, His name is Jesus and the more I get to know Him, the bigger He becomes!"[2]

The more you get to know Jesus, the more you realise there is to know. He is brilliant, inspiring and massive all at the same time.

"... they were astonished and took note that these men had been with Jesus!" (Acts 4:13). Spending time

with Jesus will always be time well spent. In a moment He can,

- Give you peace
- Provide a solution
- Help you forgive those who have hurt you
- Show you the way forward
- Help you with a choice you need to make
- Make you feel OK about yourself
- Fill you so full of purpose that you can hardly contain it.

He can do it in moment – the question is, do you have a moment?

Have you noticed how often the name of "Jesus" is used as a swear word? When a builder hits his thumb, he doesn't scream out "Mohamed", or when your classmates fall down the stairs, have you ever heard them yell, "Oh Buddha!" You will never hear a footballer scream "Mahatma Ghandi!" The reason that the name of Jesus is used in such a derogatory way is that the devil knows that there is power in name of Jesus, and so he is intent on undermining that name wherever possible.

In Acts 4:12 it says,

> *"Salvation is found in no one else, for* ***there is no other name*** *under heaven given to men by which we must be saved."*
>
> (emphasis added)

Someone once said,

> "If our greatest need had been information, God would have sent us an educator. If our greatest need was technology, God would have sent a scientist. If our greatest need was money, God would have sent a banker. If our greatest need was fun, God would have sent an entertainer. But our greatest need was forgiveness, so God sent us a Saviour, Jesus Christ!"[3]

There is no one greater than Jesus, and this Revolution is all about HIM!

Perhaps it's time to give Him a moment – this is His revolution!

5. It's Our Revolution

The stories found in church history are staggering – but, that was *then*, this is *now*. The news is: "IT'S OUR TURN NOW!" It is:

- ***Our turn*** to stand up for God and make the nation great again!
- ***Our turn*** to build nation-shaking youth groups and churches.
- ***Our turn*** to go into our schools, universities and workplaces with the Word of God on our lips.
- ***Our turn*** to be more generous than ever before.
- ***Our turn*** to be *bold, daring, dangerous, cheeky, fearless, unrestrained by convention, spirited and original.*

For the sake of 60 million people across the UK, and 450 million Europeans who need to know about Jesus, "It's Our Turn Now!"

Sean Covey warns us,

> "You'll never leave footprints in the sand by sitting on your butt, and who wants to leave butt prints in the sands of time?"[7]

... it's time to join the revolution!

Notes

1. Source: David Barrett, "Church Growth" statistician.
2. Peter Lewis, *The Glory of Christ*, Hodder & Stoughton, 1992, p. 1.
3. Author unknown.
4. Sean Covey, *Seven Habits of Highly Effective Teens*, Simon & Schuster, 1998.

Ten Steps to Being Audacious for God

The dictionary got it right. Audacious revolutionaries are

- *Bold*
- *Fearless*
- *Cheeky*
- *Daring*
- *Dangerous*
- *Unrestrained by convention*
- *Spirited* and
- *Original*

But what do those actually look like? How can you be the "Revolutionary" God has called you to be? It's time to read through the "Revolutionary Profile".

Have you got what it takes to be a revolutionary?

Step #1

Revolutionaries Know What Time It Is

Audacious revolutionaries are bold and cheeky enough to ask the question, "Who says it can't be done? Who says that one church, one youth group or one individual can't impact our nation?"

Revolutionaries know that the result of the "Super being added to our Natural" (Acts 1:8), is that, like in Acts 13:44, *"Almost the whole city gathered to hear the word of the Lord."*

Revolutionaries ask, "Why can't there be traffic jams on Sundays because of the volume of people flocking to our churches?" Revolutionaries want to know why the media continues to report that "Young people are leaving the church in massive numbers." The Revolutionaries don't understand that statement because young people are "flocking" to their churches and youth groups.

The revolutionaries understand that God is an "Audacious God" and He is raising up an Audacious generation who will be bold and fearless enough to believe that *"everything is possible for him who believes"* (Mark 9:23)

The revolutionaries are inspired by the story of Daniel in the Old Testament and know why "Now is the time to be Audacious!"

Read Daniel 1:1–21.

In the story of Daniel, chapter 1, things weren't going well for Daniel. He hadn't chosen to go to Babylon – he had been part of the Royal Family in his homeland. King Nebuchadnezzar had taken Daniel against his will. He was a prisoner of war – and there was no Geneva Convention to control how he was treated!

Your school may not be the school of your choice. Equally your home-town, job, university, family, even church may not be what you would choose. But the life of Daniel teaches us that there is no better time than now to live an Audacious Lifestyle! Daniel and his friends didn't run away from their situation when they were taken to Babylon. They didn't wait until things were in their favour before living audaciously. They simply lived the lifestyle required of a child of God.

There are 4 reasons why "Now is the time to be Audacious!"

1. You Are Part of the Royal Family

In Daniel 1:3 and 6 it says,

> *"Then the king ordered Ashpenaz, chief of his court officials, to bring in some of the Israelites from the royal family and the nobility . . . Among these were some from Judah: Daniel . . . "*

Daniel was Royalty! You are too!

In 1 Peter 2:9 it says,

> *"But you are a chosen people,* ***a royal priesthood,*** *a holy nation, a people belonging to God, that you may declare the praises of him who called you out of darkness into his wonderful light."*
>
> (emphasis added)

When King Louis of France was sent to the guillotine, his son was taken and imprisoned. His captors decided that his son would be of far greater service alive than dead. They sought to make him a puppet king, a servant to the wishes of those who could control him. He who could control the king, could effectively rule France. His captors set out to corrupt Louis' son and so surrounded him with every form of wickedness: corruption, prostitution, lies, addiction and greed! But despite tempting him with everything that France had to offer, Louis' son refused to take part in any wicked act. Through his whole time of imprisonment, he stayed pure in every way. In frustration his captors said, "We have surrounded you with all the tempting vices we can find to offer you. Why do you refuse to take part in any of this wickedness?" In reply, Louis' son said, "Because I was born to be the King!"

According to the Bible, you were born to be Royal. Royalty becomes your birthright when you step into relationship with Jesus. You can be Audacious because you were born to be so!

2. You Are in the King's Service

In Daniel 1:18–20 we read that,

> "*... at the end of the time set by the king,* [Daniel] *entered the king's service ...*'

Revolutionaries realise what time it is, because they understand that they are in the King's Service!

What would happen if you changed your perspective on life and realised that, whilst you may be at school or work, you are actually in disguise? You are really working in the "King's Service"!

The results would be staggering:

- You would no longer follow crowd, you'd lead it
- You would not be tossed around by every trend and thought, you'd be fixed and full of purpose
- When you fell down, you would get back up
- When you made a mistake, you would move on!

You're on a mission = the King's Service! The Quest is to make Him famous. You are unstoppable because you have friends in high places.

Get this, ***"The KING has a purpose for your life!"***

It doesn't matter who you are or what your job is, the King's Service needs your attention!

Alexander the Great was a great leader. He was known to walk around his army camps at night, checking on the morale of his soldiers and encouraging them to fight well the next day. On one particular occasion, Alexander the Great stumbled upon a soldier who was sleeping whilst on sentry duty: a crime punishable by death! General Alexander woke the soldier. When the soldier realised that he had been asleep and that General Alexander had discovered him, he feared for his life and began to tremble.

Alexander the Great shouted, "What's your name, soldier?" to which the soldier stammered, "My name is Alexander, sir!" Taken aback by the fact that this soldier had the same name as he did, General Alexander thought for a while and replied, "Then either change your name or stay awake!" Alexander the Great did not want his name to be associated with such inappropriate behaviour.

If you are a Christian, you are by definition someone who carries the name of Christ with you at all times! Audacious revolutionaries realise that they must be about the King's service or else change their names!

3. You Are Needed

Nebuchadnezzar was the king. That meant he could have and do anything he wanted. Although that sounds great in theory, not everything was going well for the king.

Daniel 4:4–8 says,

> *"I, Nebuchadnezzar, was at home in my palace, contented and prosperous. I had a dream that made me afraid. As I was lying in my bed, the images and visions that passed through my mind terrified me. So I commanded that all the wise men of Babylon be brought before me to interpret the*

dream for me. When the magicians, enchanters, astrologers and diviners came, I told them the dream, but they could not interpret it for me. ***Finally, Daniel came into my presence*** *and I told him the dream . . . "* (emphasis added)

The king had everything he could want, both physically and emotionally, but something was missing. Something made him afraid. There are times in every person's life when they fear something. It may be bad news, illness or even the thought of death.

When the king needed the most help and could find no-one suitable, he declared: *"Finally Daniel came into my presence . . . "* The king knew that he could get all he needed when Daniel came into the room. Daniel didn't set out to become someone's *"finally"*. He had been part of the royal family, and then he was a prisoner. He lost everything he loved and even ended up in a lions' den. But, he became someone's "finally".

What do people say when you walk in the room? Do they say, "Oh no, not him again!" or "FINALLY, you have arrived. Where have you been?"

In your school or workplace you will meet people who act full of bravado, while actually being full of questions about life. Who will be their "finally", if not you? When your friends are hurting and terrified by life, will you be their "finally"?

Revolutionaries understand that they are "needed by

someone". They understand that to be "Audacious" means to be "original". Revolutionaries don't try to be someone else. They understand that they are the answer to someone's question. They are on the planet to hear people say, "I was lost in sin and life – but FINALLY you told me about the King!"

4. Extreme Days Require Extreme Measures

One of the definitions of Audacious is "Unrestrained by Convention!" Convention is best defined as "the way things are done" or "that which is deemed acceptable".

Someone once said about the church of God, "We will not have a greater impact by doing what we have always done." In other words, *extreme days require extreme measures.*

Alexander the Great was focused on conquering the civilised world. At one point during his conquest, he reached a city which had vast, thick walls and an army of men nestled on them ready to defend the city against Alexander and his men. Alexander demanded that the king of the city surrender and let the city be won peacefully. The king laughed in response, demanding to know why Alexander would think that the city would surrender without a fight. The king said, "I have a walled city with enough provisions to last years. I have experienced fighting men on the walls. Why should I surrender to you?"

Alexander replied, "I'll show you why!" He then marched 100 men in single file off the edge of a nearby cliff. One by one the men fell to their death, without questioning the orders of their general. The history books record that the king of the city was so impressed by the soldiers' commitment to die for the vision of their general, that he opened the city gates and allowed the soldiers to enter without any more loss of life.

Alexander knew that a siege on such a walled city would involve great loss of life. An extreme situation required extreme measures!

With 19 million young people in Britain and 450 million in Europe who don't know Jesus, "Extreme days require extreme measures!"

Your Summary

Write your thoughts about this chapter here. Now is the right time for you to be a revolutionary! What do you need to do about it?

Tell everyone I possibly can, and use all the opportunities God gives me.

Step #2

Revolutionaries Are Trouble Causers!

In Acts 13:44 we read that, *"Almost the whole city* [Antioch Pisidia] *gathered to hear the word of the Lord."*

In Acts 15, we read about Paul and Barnabas arguing.

In Acts 16, Paul and Silas are involved in an amazing jail break.

And then in Acts 17:5–9 we read:

> *"But the Jews were jealous, so they rounded up some bad characters from the marketplace, formed a mob and started a riot in the city. They rushed to Jason's house in search of Paul and Silas in order to bring them out to the crowd. But when they did not find them, they dragged Jason and some other brothers before the city officials, shouting: '**These men who have caused trouble all over the world have now come here**, and Jason has welcomed them into his house. They are all defying Caesar's decrees, saying that there is another king, one called Jesus.' When they heard this, the crowd and the city officials were thrown into turmoil. Then they made Jason and the others post bond and let them go."*

(emphasis added)

Paul wasn't the type to tip-toe through the tulips. When people saw him coming, they didn't say, "What a nice lad Paul is!" In fact the opposite was true. Listen again:

> *"These men who have caused trouble all over the world have now come here* [and we don't know what to do with them!]."

Trouble

trouble (trŭb'əl)

Meaning: to

- ***agitate***
- ***disturb***
- ***afflict***
- ***annoy***

The passage effectively reads, "These people who have, agitated, disturbed, afflicted and annoyed people all over the world have now come here!" and these guys were the first Christians on the planet!

Before you go running off to play practical jokes and create a menace in school and society, there are a few things you have to understand regarding "Trouble". Paul and Silas didn't cause trouble for sake of it! They were not Bart Simpson in disguise looking for a Millhouse to wedgy, or a Moe to call, or a principal Skinner to play jokes on. They caused trouble simply because they made the decision: "We're going to live for God!"

When you live for God you naturally begin to cause trouble, even without going to look for it! If you want to be rebellious (meaning to "go against the flow"), be a Christian. Everyone else is going to hell, so why not be different and go to heaven? You get to agitate, annoy and irritate people who think going to hell is cool! You get to say, "NO! That's stupid!" Now, that's bound to get a response!

In Acts 17, people are not saying, "Paul is a nice lad. Boring, but nice."

They are saying, "That man is Dangerous! When he sings, walls fall down, and as for Peter, even his shadow makes sick people get better! They are dangerous, we can't work them out! They don't fit into a nice 'Christian' box!"

So too, with Jesus. People did not say, "He's lovely. He wears nice sandals, and isn't His beard beautifully trimmed!" They were saying, "He does freaky things – He surfs without a board (Matthew 14). He even wants us to eat His body and drink His blood (Matthew 26). He's dangerous! He casts out demons, raises the dead and He even spits!"

Dorothy Sayers writes,

> "The people who hanged Christ never ... accused Him of being a bore; on the contrary, they thought Him too dynamic to be safe ... To those who knew [Jesus], He in no way suggested a milk-and-water person; they objected to Him as a dangerous firebrand ... He insulted respectable clergymen by calling them hypocrites; He referred to King Herod as 'that fox'; He went to parties

> with disreputable company and was looked upon as being a 'gluttonous' man and a wine bibber, a friend of publicans ... He assaulted indignant tradesmen and threw them and their belongings out of the temple, He drove a horse and coaches through a number of sacrosanct and hoary regulations, He cured diseases by any means that came handy, with a shocking casualness in the matter of other people's pigs and property ... Jesus was emphatically not a dull man!"[1]

It's time to rise up as a revolutionary, and imitate THE REVOLUTIONARY – Jesus. Begin to cause trouble.

Time for a story about me. When I was just sixteen, I was learning the art of "Causing trouble God's way!" I was in college studying Sociology and had the pleasure of being taught by a woman who was an atheist and feminist! (As I was a Christian and a guy, I was the epitome of everything she hated.) When we began to study Christianity, she adopted the "scowl" position, looked in my direction and declared, "Christians believe that if you don't believe that Jesus was the Son of God and put your faith in Him, you will go to hell! Hell is a lake of fire – and you will be there forever!" She then turned to me and said, "Glyn, you are a Christian. Do you think all your classmates will go to hell?"

Needless to say, at that point I had the undivided attention of all my classmates! My class was very multi-cultural and therefore multi-faith based.

Well, what should I say? Could I run away? Could I pretend I was ill? I knew I couldn't do either of those things, so I just smiled at my class and said, "The Bible says, 'There is only one way we can be saved, and that is through Jesus.' The Bible says that the choice is open for us all and that we are responsible for the decision we make. The reality of heaven and hell is a Bible truth that I believe in and, YES, if any of my friends die without having believed in Jesus as their Lord and Saviour, they will go to hell!"

There was a pause in the classroom and then all hell broke loose! People were trying to strangle me, others were yelling obscenities at me and my teacher had a wry smile on her face. I had just caused some trouble – I didn't go looking for it – it found me! After class I thanked my teacher. She was taken aback somewhat by my politeness and asked why I was thanking her. I replied, "Because today you helped me to share my faith with all my class in a way that could have taken months and months! They know that they have a hole inside them in the shape of Jesus, and I'm believing that each of them will find faith in the God of the Bible!" Her face was a picture!

There are four things that trouble-causers do.

1. Make Other People Jealous

In Acts 17:5 it says, *"But the Jews were jealous . . . "* The leaders were jealous of Paul and the Christians because they were witnessing the "blessing" of God on their lives. People should be jealous of you and of your lifestyle!

The majority of people in our nation believe that Christianity is boring. How can that be? The Bible is amazing. Jesus is outrageous and our Father in heaven is incredible. But the reality is, people think Christianity is boring because many Christians look miserable, many churches are no happier than a funeral parlour, and some denominations are based more on legalistic principles than a "God-inspired" relationship!

People think that God is boring because often those who call themselves Christians lead boring lives.

This is not because God wants them to, but because church has often taught values, principles and laws that have been based on the premise of, "Gentle Jesus, meek and mild". The reality is that Jesus was gentle and meek at times, but He was also so dangerous that they had to kill Him. His earliest followers were also dangerous men and women.

Jesus lived such an amazing life and inspired His followers in such an overwhelming way that when people watched the early Christians, they couldn't help but be jealous of their lifestyle. Lifestyle is not just about material possessions – it's about what you do with what you have.

The church and the people within it are God's best advertisement. When the tragedy of 9/11 happened in 2001 in New York, many Christians worldwide received telephone calls from friends who were ringing to talk about issues such as life after death and the reality of God. Why were so many Christians being telephoned by people who didn't know God? Simply because, when people begin to think about God and eternity, they don't really have images of a "great God-like being", floating in space, wearing grandma's night dress and sandals. In reality, they connect God with people whom they know to be Christians. The challenging question is, when people see you and the way you live, how does that make God look? What will they think about God based on your lifestyle?

2. Trouble-Causers Defy Convention

In Acts 17:7 it says, *"They are all defying Caesar's decrees . . . "*

The word "convention" means, "status quo, doing what other people do" or "culture". Imagine if you were to announce a new, exciting youth activity called *mental head.* It involves banging your head against a wall to loud music, until you became violently, physically ill. Most people would stare at you like you were a crazy person. However, every week in our nation, we have the following scenario unfolding:

- Work hard for 5–6 days.
- Spend a lot of that hard-earned money on alcohol and drink until you are physically ill.
- Have a violent headache the next morning.
- Not remember exactly where you were the night before or what you did.
- Wonder where you contracted that sexually transmitted disease.

- Consider it a *"most excellent night out"*.

DJs and stars in the media rave about nights like this and then have the audacity to ask us to join them. There are many reasons why Revolutionaries don't get involved in that type of lifestyle. Some such reasons are integrity, holiness and simply common sense. But another reason is because in doing so, you are defying convention. Just because they are doing it, you don't have to. Revolutionaries "defy convention"!

Society creates a box and says, "Do this, go there and be like that!" The Bible says, "[God] *is able to do immeasurably more than all we ask or imagine . . .*" (Ephesians 3:20). In other words, God is not confined to a box. So when society compels you to, "Do this, say that, and go there," you can respond with an attitude that says, "Why? I'm not living in your box. It's too small for God and its 'way small' for me!"

You were born to defy convention and cause trouble. You don't have to get drunk, take drugs, have sex before marriage and get sucked in by an image that the world portrays as being good for you, when it actually only "*. . . leads to destruction*" (Matthew 7:13).

In school, university and work, people may talk about your lifestyle more than anyone else's. They may encourage or tease you to sleep around, get drunk and break the law. They may mock you or have a laugh at your expense. In reality, you are making them jealous. They wouldn't be talking about you if they didn't want to be you. Secretly, many of your friends wish they had your courage, to stand up for their convictions like you stand up for yours.

The truth is simple, perhaps even arrogant: *Don't become like them – because secretly they want to be you!*

3. Trouble Causers Serve ONE King – Jesus!

Back in the days of the Roman Empire, the citizens and conquered peoples had many gods. But their most powerful god was Caesar himself. To the Romans, he was a god in human form. To say that there was another king *above* Caesar was a crime punishable by death, and so when the Jews declared that, "[Paul and his friends were] *saying that there is another king, one called Jesus*" (Acts 17:7), it was a very serious accusation against Paul. Paul and his friends were putting their lives on the line, living all-out for King Jesus!

In reality, there are only two kings: King Jesus and king the devil. What have the two kings done for you?

King the devil has brought sin, pain, death and heartache into the world.

King Jesus has given you life, breath, friends, fun, eternity, hope. He saw the destruction the devil had caused and in return He took your sin upon Himself!

In my book, *If I Was the Devil*, I told the following story to describe what the devil really does with you:

> My best mate is called Lee. Lee and I grew up together in Australia; same street, same school,

same youth group, same church, same Bible College, same girlfriends (kidding!)

At one particular time in our friendship, I remember Lee running into my room with a grin on his face and a look of love in his eyes. When I asked him what was going on, he replied, 'I'm in love!' Now, Lee wasn't one for falling in and out of love, so this was big news! When I asked him who the poor, unfortunate soul was, he replied, 'Who else, but Fiona!' (Not really her name, but for the sake of anonymity and my desire not to get sued, we'll keep her real name a secret!)

When He shared her name with me, I nearly fell off the chair! 'Fiona? You've got to be joking!' *I felt like saying,* 'She looks a little like a barn door, is a gossip, a nag, and to make matters worse, she sometimes looks like she has two bearded men in a headlock!' (Forgive me, but I was young and prone to unpleasant thoughts at times! I know my thinking was wrong and cruel! I'm sorry!) That's what I was thinking, *but I said*, 'Fiona? That's fantastic! She's a lovely girl. I think you should take time to get to know her a little bit more – in a group, maybe – before you start going out with her!'

He replied – 'Good idea!' at which point he walked off singing 'The weather outside is frightful, but the fire is so delightful', which really didn't make sense because it was Australia and 34 degrees Celsius in the shade! Yep, he had certainly gone mad!

A few weeks later, Lee ran into my room, threw a book at my head and proceeded to pin me up against a wall whilst throwing punches into my stomach! When he calmed down I said, 'What are you doing, Poo?' (That was his nickname and that has a funny story too.) He said, 'I can't believe it!'

'What?' I replied. To which he shouted, 'Fiona! She –

- Looks a little like a barn door! (I said, 'I know')
- Is a gossip (I said, 'I know')
- A nag (I said, 'I know')
- And to make matters worse, sometimes she looks like she has two bearded men in a headlock!' (I said, 'I know')

To which he shouted, 'So, why didn't you tell me all that when I first asked you?' I answered, 'I thought it would just be a good laugh!'

Can you believe that! So much for friendship! I was in it for the laugh, and this was my mate's life we were dealing with.

That pretty much reminds me of the devil. He doesn't care about you at all. In fact, he hates you more that you can ever imagine. His sole desire is to destroy your soul and leave it desolate. He screams at you, 'Do whatever the hell you want to do, because that's where I want to take you!' He says, 'There are no rules, no rights and no wrongs – do anything you want.' And the truth is even scarier than this ... we do!"[2]

King Jesus, however, says, "Wait. There's a better way to live life than that!" There may be two kings, but there is only one KING!

4. Trouble Causers Get a Name for Themselves

Acts 17:6 says, *"These men who have caused trouble all over the world have now come here . . . "*

Everyone has a reputation. We are all known by our friends and acquaintances for some reason. Recently in the USA, a radio station wanted to test out this theory, so whilst on air, they telephoned businesses at random and asked to speak to "Dumb Bum". They discovered, much to the delight and amusement of thousands of listeners, that a large percentage of receptionists and staff would reply in the following ways:

- "He's not at the desk at the moment"
- "Sure, I'll just put you through to Emma"
- "Which one would you like to speak to?"

Every school has its nerd, its bully and its hairy yeti. Everyone has a reputation for something!

What are you known for? Paul's reputation in the Bible is summarised in verse 6, he *". . . caused trouble all over the world."*

In Acts 19, we read the amazing story of the seven sons of Sceva who tried, unsuccessfully, to cast demons out of people in the name of Jesus. A demon spoke to them saying, "Jesus I know, and I know about Paul, but who are you?" (Acts 19:15). The demons knew who Paul was! Your reputation is not just known on earth!

There are three areas where it is worth getting a "decent" reputation:

i. Get known in hell!

Wouldn't it be fascinating if hell began to get nervous every time you woke up! If you walked onto "hell's turf" and hell screamed "Get off our patch," you replied with an attitude and lifestyle that yells, "No, you get off my patch. If you got a problem, talk to my King!"

Some people wrongly create a divide between their spiritual life and their natural life. People believe that Sunday is spiritual because you "do the church thing" and Monday in natural because you "do the work thing". The reality is that if you have relationship with God, then everything you do is spiritual.

The word secular means "void of God". The moment you walk into a place that is secular, it immediately stops being void of God, because you took God with you into that situation!

Make hell tremble at the very mention of your name, because you live such a righteous life!

ii. Get known in heaven

With reality TV becoming a major influence in the early part of the new millennium, people have became transfixed by watching other people "do life". Similarly, earth is heaven's reality TV! Heaven is currently watching your life! (see Hebrews 12:1).

Heaven is switched on to your life right now, awaiting the next episode! If your life had "ratings" according to how many heaven-dwellers were watching you, just think how many of them would be tuned into you with great excitement, wondering what you were going to do for God next.

iii. Get known in your environment

It would be amazing if people in your school, university or work place began to say, "Hey, there's something different about you. I can't quite work you out, you don't fit in the Christian box that I had you placed in."

How much more amazing if your attitude was, "I am a danger to anyone who is comfortable with the thought of going hell! I am going to annoy you, disturb you and agitate you as far as I can without getting the sack in the process!"

Acts 16:35–37 says,

> *"When it was daylight, the magistrates sent their officers to the jailer with the order: 'Release those men.' The jailer told Paul, 'The magistrates have ordered that you and Silas be released. Now you can leave. Go in peace.' But Paul said to the officers: 'They beat us publicly without a trial, even though we are Roman citizens, and threw us into prison. And now do they want to get rid of us quietly? No! Let them come themselves and escort us out.'"*

What an amazing passage. That attitude read today would say, "We won't stand by and watch a generation and world go to hell. It's time to cause trouble!"

Both heaven and hell are waiting with bated breath for the outcome of your life! Why not make heaven proud?!

It's time to cause trouble. It's time to get dangerous!

Your Summary

In Job 14:1 it says, *"Man . . . is of few days and full of trouble!"* If that's the case, then make trouble for a righteous cause! Write your thoughts about this chapter here and what you need to do to in order to cause a bit of trouble.

Notes

1. Quoted by Mal Fletcher in *The Pioneer Spirit*, Next Wave International, p. 32.
2. Glyn Barrett, *If I Was the Devil*, Sovereign World, p. 26.

Step #3

Revolutionaries Know How to Live Amazing Lives!

> *"Therefore, since we have a great high priest who has gone through the heavens, Jesus, the Son of God, let us hold firmly to the faith we profess. For we do not have a high priest who is unable to sympathize with our weaknesses, but we have one who has been tempted in every way, just as we are – yet was without sin. Let us then approach the throne of grace with confidence, so that we may receive mercy and find grace to help us in our time of need."*
>
> (Hebrews 4:14–16)

Revolutionaries are amazing people because they understand that:

- Life is short, death is sure, sin is a curse and Jesus is the cure ... and so they commit themselves to living amazing lives!

In the Rugby World Cup Final in 2003, the whole nation of England was jumping around shouting "We Won, We Won, We Won!" – but the reality is ... THEY (the team) won; we (the nation) just watched!

In life, you can either be a spectator and watch the world pass you by, or you can really commit yourself to living an amazing life. There is no better feeling than putting your head on the pillow at night and saying, "Today, I really lived well!"

So, how do you live an amazing life? There are five ways:

1. Keep Choosing God

Hebrews 4:14 refers to Jesus as the "... *great high priest ... Jesus the Son of God.*" What you've got to understand about Jesus is that He's BIG!

- The Bible doesn't say He is the King; He is the KING OF KINGS
- The Bible doesn't say He is the Lord; He is the LORD OF LORDS
- The Bible doesn't say He is Peace; He is the PRINCE OF PEACE
- He's not "a" way; He's "THE" WAY
- He's not "a" truth; He's "THE" TRUTH
- He's not "a" life; He's "THE" LIFE
- He's not "a" priest; He's "THE GREAT HIGH PRIEST"

If you have Jesus as your greatest friend, you have a friend in high places.

In the movie *Bear*, an orphaned bear cub was adopted by a grizzly bear in the wild. The big grizzly bear taught the cub how to hunt fish and to defend itself. In one particular scene, the little cub was on its own, when a cougar began to circle him, presumably to kill and eat him. The little cub remembered what the grizzly had taught it and managed a tiny little growl to scare off the predator – but the noise from the little cub was almost laughable. The cougar advanced on its prey. When the little cub let out another timid little growl, to the audience's amazement, the cougar turned around and fled for its life. As the camera panned around, it showed the little cub, with a look of surprise and pride on its face. As the camera continued to pan further, it showed the big grizzly standing behind the cub; tall and fierce. The cougar wasn't really afraid of the cub – he was petrified of the bear behind him!

The devil may not be all that afraid of you – but he is petrified of the guy standing behind you! Jesus is MASSIVE! The Bible calls him the "LION OF THE TRIBE OF JUDAH"! When you go into school or work, you don't go in as "little-old-you" with just nothing, you go with a friend in high places. In fact you can't get a higher place and higher name than that of Jesus.

God has a track record that spans back to the creation of the world! In school, track record is everything! Perhaps in nursery and primary school there was a bully who used to push you around. Perhaps when you saw him coming, you ran the other way. Perhaps by the time you went to secondary school, that bully had the reputation of being the toughest kid in school, until the day he picked a fight with a girl, who whipped him in the fight and broke his nose. In a moment, the bully went from being known as the "tough kid" to having a track record that said, "You're the dude that got beat up by a girl!"

God has an amazing track record! He says:

- "Creation? I did that!"
- "I pummelled Pharaoh"
- "I whooped the Philistines"
- "I helped Gideon and Joshua"
- "I came to earth"
- "I stood on the devil"
- "I made you"
- "I even helped Gilligan get off the Island"???!

In the Old Testament, we read that God is, *"The LORD, the God of your fathers – the God of Abraham, Isaac, Jacob . . . "* (Exodus 3:16). God has an amazing track record and what He was saying was, "If I can do great things for them, I can do them for you!"

Think about your greatest spiritual hero for a moment. Maybe it's your youth pastor, your pastor, a friend, or a minister you know from a distance. Whatever God has done for them – their track record – He can do for you, AND MORE!

2 Corinthians 9:15 says, *"Thanks be to God for his indescribable gift* [of Jesus Christ]*!"* It's impossible to put into words what Jesus has done for us. So instead, you put it into "life action". Joshua put it this way,

> *"Now fear the LORD and serve him with all faithfulness. Throw away the gods your forefathers worshipped beyond the River and in Egypt, and serve the LORD. But if serving the LORD seems*

undesirable to you, then choose for yourselves this day whom you will serve, whether the gods your forefathers served beyond the River, or the gods of the Amorites, in whose land you are living. But as for me and my household, we will serve the L*ORD*.''
(Joshua 24:14–16)

2. Keep Your Eye on Eternity

Hebrews 4:14 says of Jesus that He has ''*. . . gone through the heavens . . .* ''

In Ecclesiastes 3:11, it says ''[God] *has also set eternity in the hearts of men.*''

In order to fly from one destination to another, you have to spend time in the airport. You have to check in your bags and get your boarding pass for the plane. You might then do some last-minute shopping because you forgot your travel plug again and then finish up with a coffee in an overpriced airport café. In the airport you will see a lot of different things, but there will be no tents with people living in them. Why? Because people don't pitch tents and live in airports!

If you are flying from Britain to Australia, you might spend three to four hours in an airport in Malaysia or Thailand, but you won't pitch tent, because you don't live there! You're en route, just passing through!

Equally, the earth is not your home! You come from the heart of God and are en route to eternity. You are just passing through this world, you are not here to live permanently. While the 70 years we may live seems like a long time, in the light of eternity, 70–80 years is really only like 3–4 hours!

The great preacher Jonathan Edwards said in his sermon "Sinners in the hands of an angry God", preached in Northampton, MA in the 1700s:

> "Unconverted men walk over the pit of hell on a rotten covering, and there are innumerable places in this covering so weak that they will not bear their weight, and these places are not seen. The arrows of death fly unseen at noon-day ... All the means that there are of sinners going out of the world, are so in God's hands, and so universally and absolutely subject to his power and determination, that it does not depend at all the less on the mere will of God, whether sinners shall at any moment go to hell, than if means were never made use of, or at all concerned in the case."[1]

Eternity is in you right now and the reality is that eternity is only one heartbeat away! When you keep your eye on eternity, it saves you from the "silly season".

In Luke 15:11–32 we read about the story of the Prodigal Son. In verse 17 it says, "*When he came to his senses ...*"

Imagine how much hassle and money he would have saved himself if he had *come* to his senses, before he was *forced* to come to his senses. He squandered, wasted, regretted, and then came to his senses. Why go through something, regret it, and *then* come to your senses? Why not come to your senses now and save yourself the heartache of messing things up?

You will have many opportunities in life to squander and waste your destiny. Keeping eternity in your heart will save you from messing things up! You can decide today, "I am not going to do what my friends are doing – I am not going to go where my friends go – I've got eternity in my heart!"

3. Live What You Say You Believe

Hebrews 4:14 says, *"Let us hold firmly to the faith we profess."*

Some people profess a faith in Jesus, but in reality don't hold firmly to it.

Two men worked together on a factory floor for twenty years. Every day they would clock in at the same time, talk about life, marriage, money, the job and then go home. They would occasionally meet up at restaurants and go on nights out, so that over the twenty year period they got to know each other pretty well. One fateful day, one of the men fell to the floor, clutching his heart, crying out in fear and pain. As his colleagues gathered around him, he panted, "Someone please get me a Christian – I need to get my life right with God!" One of the workers asked if anyone there was a Christian, but no-one stepped forward.

Sadly, the man passed away that morning. His workmates gathered for his funeral a few days later, and after the ceremony, one of the workers approached the dead man's friend and said, "You are a Christian. I see you go to church every Sunday. Why didn't you step forward when your friend was asking for a Christian?" There was no reply, so he asked again, to which the worker sadly replied, "I couldn't step forward as a Christian, because my life closed my lips."

He was a man who professed a faith in Jesus (if only on Sundays and at home), but didn't have the conviction to hold firmly to the faith he professed; to live it out daily.

Perhaps for some time you have been at school, university or work and people there don't know you are a Christian. It's time to "hold firmly to the faith you profess".

Living an amazing life involves "nailing your colours to the mast", making and living a life that says, "I live for the cause of Jesus Christ – I am not ashamed to say it and I'm not embarrassed to live it!" Living for Him often means going against popular consensus and opinion.

Nailing your colours to the mask can be a scary thing; the fear of ridicule can be so overwhelming that it overcomes the desire to stand for God. But Hebrews 4:16 says *"Let us approach the throne of grace with confidence . . . "* This is a very reassuring verse for those wanting to nail their colours to the mast! It's truth is played out in the following story:

During the Civil War in the America, a young soldier in the Union Army lost his older brother and his father in the battle of Gettysburg. The soldier decided to go to Washington, D.C. to see President Lincoln to ask for exemption from military service so that he could go back and help his sister and mother with the spring planting on their farm. When he arrived in Washington, having received a furlough to plead his case, he went to the White House, approached the front gate and asked to see the President.

The guard on duty told him, "You can't see the President, young man! Don't you know there's a war going on? The President is a very busy man! Now go away! Get back out there on the battle lines where you belong!"

The young soldier left feeling disheartened. As he sat on a little park bench not far from the White House, a little boy came up to him. The lad said, "Soldier, you look unhappy. What's wrong?" The soldier looked at the little boy and began to spill his heart to him. He told of his father and brother being killed in the war, and of the desperate situation at home. He explained that his mother and sister had no one to help them with the farm. The little boy listened and said, "I can help you, soldier." He took the soldier by the hand and led him back to the front gate of the White House. Apparently, the guard didn't notice them, because they weren't stopped. They went straight up to the front door of the White House and walked right in! After they got inside, they walked right past the generals and high ranking officials, and no one said a word. The soldier couldn't understand this. Why didn't anyone try to stop them?

Finally they reached the oval office where the President was working, and the little boy didn't even knock on the door. He just walked right in and led the soldier in with him. There behind the desk was

Abraham Lincoln and his Secretary of State, looking over battle plans that were laid out on his desk.

The President looked at the boy and then at the soldier and said, "Good afternoon Todd. Can you introduce me to your friend?"

Todd Lincoln, the son of the President, said, "Daddy, this soldier needs to talk to you."

The soldier pleaded his case before Mr. Lincoln, and, right then and there he received the exemption he had desired.[2]

When you nail your colours to the mast, you have to KNOW, that you have straight access to the "big guy" stood behind you. In a moment of panic, embarrassment or frustration, a simple prayer will lift your spirits and give you the courage you need to make sure that your life doesn't close your lips!

4. Spend Your Life for Others

Re-reading Hebrews 4:14–16 will show that 11 times it says "us", "we" or "our". The most famous verse in the Bible is John 3:16 which says,

> *"For God so loved the world, that he gave his one and only Son, that* ***whoever*** *believes in him shall not perish but have eternal life."*
>
> (emphasis added)

The King James version uses the word "whosoever". Have you noticed that church is full of whosoevers?

Weird people who you would not usually mix with if you had your choice. If you were in school or work together, you wouldn't naturally gravitate to them – because they are just too weird! But somehow, you end up with them in church! The truth is, "Everybody is someone else's weirdo"! You may think the guy in front of you in church is strange, but the guy behind you thinks you are absolutely nuts!

Life is not and never has been all about you! It's about all the whosoevers that you find yourself around! Revolutionaries spend their lives on others, because Jesus died for the "whosoever" and for the world (John 3:16).

Fiorello LaGuardia was the Mayor of New York City during the worst days of the Great Depression and throughout all of WWII. He was loved by many New Yorkers who called him the "Little Flower" because of his name and the fact that he was so short and wore a carnation in his lapel.

He would ride the New York City fire trucks, raid city "speak-easies" with the police department, took entire orphanages to baseball games and, when the New York newspapers went on strike, he got on the radio and read the Sunday "funnies" to the city's children.

On one cold night in January 1935, the mayor turned up at a night court that served the poorest part of the city. LaGuardia dismissed the judge for the evening and took over the bench himself. Within a few minutes, a tattered old woman was brought before him, charged with stealing a loaf of bread. She told LaGuardia that her daughter's husband had deserted her, her daughter was sick, and her two grandchildren were starving.

But the shopkeeper, from whom the bread was stolen, refused to drop the charges. "It's a real bad neighborhood, your Honor," the man told the Mayor. "She's got to be punished to teach other people around here a lesson."

LaGuardia sighed. He turned to the woman and said, "I've got to punish you. The law makes no exceptions. Pay ten dollars or ten days in jail." But even as he pronounced sentence, the Mayor was already reaching into his pocket. He extracted a bill and tossed it into his famous hat, saying, "Here is the ten dollar fine which I now remit; and furthermore, I am going to fine everyone in this courtroom fifty cents for living in a town where a person has to steal bread so that her grandchildren can eat. Mr. Bailiff, collect the fines and give them to the defendant."

The following day, New York City newspapers reported that $47.50 was turned over to a bewildered woman who had stolen a loaf of bread to feed her starving grandchildren. Fifty cents of that amount was contributed by the grocery store owner himself, while petty criminals, people with traffic violations, and New York City policemen, each of whom had just paid fifty cents for the privilege of doing so, gave the Mayor a standing ovation.[3]

The Mayor of the city made a choice to "spend his life, living for others". That's what Jesus did when He left heaven to come to earth 2,000 years ago. He chose to live for us so that we could benefit from His life. Revolutionaries understand that they are on the planet so that others can benefit from their lives.

5. Do Something!

The true story of Larry Walters tells us what we need to do in order to live "amazing lives"!

A few years ago 33-year-old truck driver Larry Walters made national news. Larry had a habit of spending his weekends in his Los Angeles backyard, just south of L.A. International Airport, drinking Pepsi and eating peanut butter sandwiches. He would sit in his favourite lawn chair staring at the houses around him in the subdivision where he lived. Not a real exciting life.

One day abject boredom prompted Larry Walters to buy some balloons and a tank of helium. He figured on tying the balloons to his lawn chair, filling them with helium, and floating up for an aerial view of the neighbourhood. He judged he'd get no higher than 100 feet, but just in case, he got out his BB gun and loaded it. He planned to regulate his altitude by shooting out a couple of balloons. I'm not sure how many six packs of Pepsi he had consumed when he came to that idea, but he decided it was worth a try.

So Larry Walters of Los Angeles went out and bought 45 big weather balloons, a huge tank of helium, and some rope. First he secured his lawn chair to the ground, then he filled the balloons with helium. One by one he tied them to his lawn chair. Before lift off he went in the house and got another six-pack of Pepsi, a couple of peanut butter and jelly sandwiches, and his BB gun. Then he went out and sat in his lawn chair. He had instructed his neighbours to cut the ropes securing the chair when he was ready. "Let's go!" he yelled, and the ropes were cut.

But he didn't go 100 feet. He went up 11,000 feet! Shot straight up in the air! And the BB gun? It was useless since he was using both hands to hang on to the chair for dear life.

He zoomed straight up into the landing pattern at L.A. Airport. The pilot of an approaching Continental DC10 reported that he had just passed a man in a lawn chair, and the control tower told him to report in immediately upon landing. They thought the pilot might have been drinking. Can you imagine being a passenger in that plane? "Look, Mum, out the window. There's a man in a lawn chair!"

Eventually they sent up helicopters to rescue Larry Walters. They closed the airport and diverted all landings and takeoffs at LAX while they played tag with this fellow in his lawn chair at 11,000 feet. When they finally got him down, he was surrounded by TV crews, the police, fire and rescue squads, and plenty of curious people. It was a major event.

"Were you scared?" asked one of the TV reporters, thrusting a mike in his face.

"No, not really" said Larry.

"Are you going to do it again?" asked another reporter.

"No," said Larry.

"What in the world made you do it the first time?"

Larry Walters thought about it for a moment and said,

"Well, you can't just sit there!"[4]

The Bible tells us that in heaven there is a book. It's called the "Lamb's Book of Life" and if your name is in that book because you have had a relationship with Jesus, then you get access to eternity with Him. What if the Lamb's Book of Life didn't only have your name in it, but your story too? Imagine that when you step up to the gates of heaven, Peter or the Archangel says, "Joe Bloggs – this is your life!"

"Joe was born in Manchester, England in 1972 ..." Peter begins and the story of your life is told. Imagine heaven applauding as it hears about when you were 12 and you made the decision that Jesus was Lord and chose to follow Him all the days of your life! Imagine the cheers when Peter quotes the date that you chose to "live an amazing, revolutionary life for Jesus". Imagine the nods of approval when you got married and when your children were born. The story goes right up to the time when you stepped off this planet and into eternity with Jesus! At which point, someone says, "Joe, because of Jesus and what He has done for you and because you chose to live life for Him ... heaven is open – come and meet your Jesus!" The host of heaven stand to their feet and applaud THE REVOLUTIONARY Jesus, for His work on the cross 2,000 years ago, securing your salvation, and then they turn to welcome you, a Revolutionary who lived to make God proud!

What will the story of your life read like? Will it be an amazing life? Or not? The stories of the revolutionaries are amazing! Heaven waits with bated breath for the next instalment of the story of your life. It hasn't been written because you are yet to write it! You can't just sit there, get up, write a great story and live amazing!

Your Summary

Write your thoughts about this chapter here and what you need to do in order to live an amazing life.

Notes

1. Jonathan Edwards, "Sinners in the hands of an angry God". See www.jonathanedwards.com/sermons/Warnings/sinners.htm.
2. Wayne Rice, *More Hot Illustrations for Youth Talks*, Zondervan, p. 140.
3. Steve Goodier, "Life Support", www.LifeSupportSystem.com.
4. Wayne Rice, *Still More Hot Illustrations for Youth Talks*, Zondervan, pp. 27–28.

Step #4

Revolutionaries Are the Head, Not the Tail

In Deuteronomy 28:13 it says:

> *"The* LORD *will make you the* ***head, not*** *the* ***tail.*** *If you pay attention to the commands of the* LORD *your God that I give you this day and carefully follow them, you will always be at the top, never at the bottom."*
>
> (emphasis added)

There are many cultures in the world which exemplify the principle of "the head and not the tail" very clearly. In Africa, there are tribes who show incredible respect to their chiefs. Often this comes in the form of bowing, kneeling, or clapping when they see the chief approaching. They stay in that act of submission until the chief either passes them by or approaches them and engages in conversation. The chief is clearly the head, *not* the tail.

So what does being the "head, not the tail" really mean? It means that we have the God-given right to rise up in any situation and begin to take a leadership role, however small, that brings change to the environment we are in.

In Matthew 16:13–20, Peter learns four key lessons on how to rise up and be a "head and not the tail" revolutionary. It is important to remember that what most people want are encounters with leaders, conferences or books and resources; but it is really only an encounter with Jesus that identifies you as a revolutionary and a person who is the "head and not the tail".

1. Don't Be a Hearsay Leader

In verse 13, Jesus asks *"Who do people say the Son of Man is?"* The response in verse 14 reads, *"Some say ... others say ... still others* [say] ... " Notice the progression: "some ... others ... still others ..."

In verse 13, Jesus wants to know what the gossip is. "What exactly are people saying?" And in verse 14, the disciples reply with the current gossip.

In verse 15, however, Jesus gets straight to the heart of the matter: *"Who do you say I am?"* In other words, "Don't be a *hearsay* leader. Don't get your understanding about me from the grapevine – What do YOU say to be true?"

Often we make hearsay the foundation of what we believe. We believe things because this man of God or that woman of God said it. We fall into the trap of adopting a leadership model or a technique that someone mentions and end up living our lives running after *"some say, others say, and still others say."*

Jesus is demanding something from Peter in

Matthew 16, "Hey Peter, don't be a hearsay leader. Don't live life based on what other people think and believe to be true. What do you say? What do you believe?"

All too often, young people base their Christianity on what they hear people say about God. Many pastors change their church structure depending on what other leaders say, so that many churches and youth groups have adopted models based on *"some say, others say and still others say."* Most leadership conferences involve hearsay and even this book is hearsay to you – it's my experience versus your experience.

Hearsay has its place if it challenges thinking, but Jesus is saying that if you want to be a revolutionary who is the "head and not the tail", then hearsay is not enough to live life on.

2. Lead from a Place of Revelation

In verse 16, Peter replies, *"You are Christ"* and Jesus answers him in verse 17, *"Blessed are you Simon . . . for this was not revealed to you by man, but by my Father in heaven."* Revolutionaries lead from a place of revelation. Even Jesus Himself lived a life based on revelation. In John 5:19, Jesus says "I only do what I see Father doing." In other words, you have to *see it in heaven and copy it on earth.*

Revelation is an unstoppable force in you. It is a word hot off the press from the heart of God via the Word of God to you. Revolutionaries assess whether they are living a life of hearsay or a life centred on revelation.

In the book *If I Was the Devil*, I recalled the first sermon I ever preached. It went something like this:

> "When I was 15, my family moved from Australia to Manchester. After a few weeks at the school, my teacher asked me to do the 'God-talk' in chapel. I was instantly flattered, and felt proud to be asked to do the job. After all, I was no longer the same 'critter' who made bombs and blew up dogs. I had definitely changed.
>
> When I got home that day, I suddenly realised, 'Oh no. Doing the "God-talk" means getting up in front of people and ... talking.' (Yes I know, I wasn't all that clever). My revelation went further when I realised that in order to talk, I had to have something to say. I suddenly had that sinking feeling in the pit of my stomach. You know, the type of feeling you get when,
>
> - Your dad says, 'I want a word with you' or ...
> - The letter arrives with your dentist appointment on,
> - You realise you just swam butt naked in front of your school ... you understand!
>
> So now I am at home, scared about what to do when I suddenly remember something. The sinking feeling gives way to the feeling of delight when I realise ... 'YES – I HAVE AN IDEA.'
>
> David Meece was a singer songwriter from America (yep, I'll admit there were times when I was him, playing air guitar – although he played

piano, which wouldn't really work, because you couldn't play air guitar with a piano, because it's too heavy, and ... never mind!) On one of his albums, he did a 7 minute preachy bit and so I decided I would nick it.

I wrote it out word for word, practised and practised, and then came the big day.

I woke up early, had that sinking feeling again, but put on David Meece and heard the way he delivered it one last time. I had a shower, played a little bit of air guitar – yep, I was looking good – now it was time.

I rode my bike to school (looked a bit windswept when I got there – but it gave me the rugged/unkempt look). I walked into the chapel service and was introduced to the school. There was applause and instantly I was taken back to air-guitar land. Yep, I had been here before.

I stood up to talk, and it was going really well. People were laughing in all the right places, as well as oohing and ahhing in all the right places too. This was good. But, it started to go pear-shaped when I mentioned that in 1968, I was driving my Buick down the main highway in Chicago (or words to that effect), and you could see people's minds begin to do some mental arithmetic. Their heads probably told them something like this,

- 'Glyn, you weren't born in 1968.'
- 'Glyn, you've never been to America.'
- 'Glyn, you can't even drive a car.'

> From that point on, I had *really gained* their attention. They knew I had made everything up. They knew I had copied someone else. In fact, my teacher said, 'Glyn, well presented, but perhaps it would be better if you were yourself and stopped trying to be like someone else.' I was so embarrassed."

The problem with that sermon was that there was no revelation, nothing fresh and hot from God on my heart that could be shared with the audience.

Revelation is all about asking, "What is God saying to me?" What is God saying to you about:

- Your friends
- Your future
- Your family
- Your school or university or workplace
- Your life?

It's only through prayer that you really begin to access revelation for your life. A preacher recently put prayer and communication with God this way:

> "Every morning I wake up, I try to spend some time with God. I'll read the part of the Bible that I am up to for the day, then I'll thank God for all that He has done and is going to do. I also bring my prayer requests before God. I pray for family, friends and even current situations. After that, I try to be quiet and listen to God to see if He is saying anything. Sometimes, He does speak

through a small whisper, an impression or through what I just read in the Bible. Other times I don't really feel impressed by anything in my 'quiet' time. So I shower, change, have breakfast with the family and drive off to work. I noticed though, that throughout the day, God begins to speak to me through various conversations, situations or even reminding me of a prophetic word or the written word. Thinking about why sometimes I don't hear God speak in the morning, but I do later on in the day can probably best be compared with emails. In the morning, I go-online with God and connect with him, then throughout the rest of the day, my heart is open and connected with heaven, and at any time God can send me a message. That message is always revelation which spurs me on and makes the day a better day ..."

Make a positive decision to go on-line with God in the morning and watch how God communicates with you more throughout the day.

3. Know God

In Matthew 16:13, Jesus asks, *"Who do people say the Son of Man is?"* In Exodus 3, God speaks to Moses (revelation) and says, "I don't want you to be a leader of sheep any more, I want you to lead people." Moses replies in verse 13, "Who shall I say sent me?" At which point God replies, *"I AM WHO I AM ... say to the*

Israelites: 'I AM has sent me to you' " (verse 14). It's a weird reply from God, but a very profound one.

In the Old Testament, when God revealed Himself to someone, He would refer to Himself by a name which represented one of His characteristics.

So He says, "I am ...

- *Jehovah Shalom* – "The Lord is my peace"
- *Jehovah Tsidkenu* – "The Lord is my righteousness"
- *Jehovah Nissi* – "The Lord is my banner"
- *Jehovah Jireh* – "The Lord is my provider" etc.

The reason God did this and allowed people to refer to Him by these names, is so that people could understand something about the greatness of God. But in Exodus chapter 3, He doesn't limit Himself to one characteristic. He is literally saying to Moses, "My ways are higher than your ways; my thoughts are higher than your thoughts ... "

- I am a shepherd, banner, love, light, provider and so many other characteristics.
- I'm not a statue. I don't fit on the end of a stick and I don't live in a building.
- I'm the God who can do immeasurably more than you can ask or imagine (Ephesians 3:20).
- *"I AM!"*

So when Jesus asked, "Who do you say I am?" Peter, although his answer was very acceptable, should have replied, "YES – you are the Great I AM."

He's not the great "I can", nor is He the great "I was". He is not even the great "I will be" – He is the great "I AM" – He just IS great!

In Psalm 119:68, it says *"You are good, and what you do is good."* In other words, "Who God is, determines what God does. He can only DO according to WHO HE IS."

The Bible says, *"God is good"* (Psalm 73:1) therefore *everything* He does is good. He is not struggle, disease, heartache or disaster – because He is good.

The Bible says *"God is great"* (Psalm 70:4 NLT) therefore *everything* He does is great. Nothing God does is small or insignificant, because He is GREAT.

The Bible says "God is faithful" (Deuteronomy 7:9). He doesn't have to work hard at being faithful, He just is.

If church is not good, great or faithful, is God really there? If a Christian is not good, great or faithful, is God really living in that person? If a Christian event is not good, where is God? He is good. Perhaps churches that represent a dull, boring, old-fashioned God should be challenged to change or even shut down, because,

- God is Good, Great and Faithful, and so is everything He does.

The point is simple: "How you know God, determines what you believe God does." If you believe God to be angry, then He's always mad and carries a big stick to beat you with. If you believe God to be vengeful, He instigates sickness, war and disease.

More so, "who" you know God to be determines

your approach to every situation. If you know your God to be good, then you'll know that in any situation, "All things will work together for good." If God is great, then no matter how big your problem, God is greater. If God is faithful, then whenever you make a mistake, He won't beat you or turn His back on you, He is faithful.

Knowing the God of the Bible is far more important than knowing the God of hearsay. Revolutionaries don't just believe what others say about God, they open their own Bibles and find God for themselves.

Revolutionaries know the God of THE BOOK – THE BIBLE. In 2 Peter 1:3 it says,

> *"His divine power has given us everything we need for life and godliness through our knowledge of him who called us by his own glory and goodness."*

You have everything you need for LIFE and GODLINESS (good living), but you have to know God, and the best way to know him is through the Bible.

4. Know Yourself

In Matthew 16:17, Jesus says, *"Blessed are you, Simon ..."* I wonder what the disciples would have been thinking when Jesus said that?

Let's explain it this way. Your name goes hand in hand with what you are known for. If your friend was to walk into your classroom and announce that you were on your way, immediately everyone in the room would begin to think of you with reference to a conversation they had with you or a way of behaving that is typically "you".

Think about some of your friends. Undoubtedly there are characteristics about them that are typically theirs alone.

The phrase "I AM" summed up who Jesus was and the name "Simon" summed up who the disciples knew Simon to be – arrogant, brash, impetuous, inconsistent.

We are all known for something. But the real question for you is: what do you want to be known for? To become renowned for something, you have to live and breathe, eat and sleep it.

- Noah is known for the Ark that he built, but it took him 120 years.
- Esther is known for being strong, but it required her putting her own life on the line.
- David is known for killing Goliath, but he had spent years perfecting the art of slingshot.

In Matthew 16:18, Jesus changes what Simon is to be known for. Jesus renames him Peter. This is profound because Simon means "reed", but Peter means "rock". A reed is blown around by the wind – which resembles Simon's impetuous behaviour – but a rock stands firm. Simon changed from impulsive to "Peter the Rock".

What are you known for? Do you know yourself? Revolutionaries realise their reputation and allow God to grow them into a new one. One that makes Him proud.

Your Summary

Write your thoughts about this chapter here, and what you need to do to in order to live like you are the head and not the tail.

Step #5

Revolutionaries Know They Are Called

I had an amazing experience when I was 12 years old. Five of my friends and I decided we wanted to discover God for ourselves. Some of us had grown up in church and had listened to hundreds of sermons and Sunday school talks, but we really wanted to know God, not based on our parent's relationships with God or our Sunday school teacher's relationship with God, but on our own.

We approached our youth pastor and asked him if we could use his office to pray each night on the following week. We had two rules for the prayer meetings:

1. Strictly no adults (what did they know anyway?)
2. Absolutely no girls (we didn't want to get distracted)

So we met and prayed for six consecutive nights. As the week continued, more and more guys our age joined to pray with us, until by the Saturday night there were about 40 of us meeting together with the purpose of meeting God.

On the Monday night, some of the guys were "baptised in the Holy Spirit" (see Acts 2). Each night that followed, more and more of the guys were also baptised in the Holy Spirit. I on the other hand was not. On the final night of prayer, when I was so desperate to know God more, He also filled me with the Holy Spirit. In that moment, God began to speak to me about what he had planned for me to do in life – it was an amazing experience.

Looking back on it now, I realise it was "the call of God" for my life. God wanted me to be a minister in church life. The "call of God" is best defined as "plans and purposes for your life". Plans are things you write down or draw and follow in order to get to a destination or achieve some desired end. A map is a plan that helps you decide your route when you are on holiday. Builders also follow a plan in order to construct a house.

In life, God has a plan and purpose for you. Jeremiah 29:11 says,

> *"'For I know the plans I have for you,' declares the LORD, 'plans to prosper you and not to harm you, plans to give you hope and a future.'"*

In Exodus 3:1–10, we read four things about "calling" that Revolutionaries understand.

1. You Were Always Called

God has been calling your name for ages. Before the world began God called your name. The Bible says in Jeremiah 1:5 *"Before I formed you in the womb I knew you, before you were born I set you apart . . . "*

The word "knew" speaks of God having been in close relationship with you "before" you were born. When God called your name, He spoke your name in the context of the plans or the path you could take, and the great purpose He has for your life. Your name has rung out for centuries because you have always been in the heart of God.

The word "opportunity" means: "break, chance, moment, occasion, opening, possibility, time". Your name has rung out awaiting the opportunity when God would say, "Now is the time, this is the moment, here is the opening for you to be put on the planet." You are no freak of nature or accident, you were planned in the heart of God since before time began, and you live now because "this is your moment".

Moses was always called. Look at his life:

- He was a baby, but he was called.
- He was an orphan, but he was called.
- He was adopted, but he was called.
- He was a prince, but he was called.
- He was a murderer, but he was called.
- He was a wanderer, but he was called.

He didn't know he was called. He just wandered until he came to a bush that was, rather strangely, on fire and talking. But he was always called.

You also have always been called by God. He has plans and purposes for your life:

- When you were a baby, you were called.
- Whether you are rich or poor ... you are called.

- Whether family life has been really tough ... you are still called.
- Perhaps you got divorced ... you are called.
- Perhaps your parents got divorced and things have been tough since then ... you are called.
- Maybe you committed a terrible crime. Guess what? Still called.
- Whoever you are, whatever has happened to you and whatever you have done, YOU ARE CALLED BY GOD.

This book could be your burning bush. As you are reading this, perhaps for the first time you are realising that God has a dream for what you can accomplish. That's an exciting dream and nothing can stop it ... well, one thing can. That thing is you choosing to do it. Nevertheless, you were always called.

2. The Call Will Draw You

Fire has an amazing effect on people. Whether it is a campfire, a coal fire in a cosy living room on a cold day, or even a house fire, they draw people's attention.

In the story in Exodus chapter 3, Moses sees a fire. In verse 4 it says, *"When the LORD saw that he had gone over to look, God called to him from within the bush, 'Moses! Moses!' And Moses said, 'Here I am.'"*

The fact that God only spoke when Moses drew near tells us two things:

1. You have to be in the right environment if you are going to hear from God. That's why it's good to go to church or youth group, because in that atmosphere of faith and expectancy, you are likely to hear God speak to you.
2. You have to take action. God only spoke to Moses when he drew (walked) near. When you read about the great miracles that Jesus did in the New Testament, it's important to note that He only healed those who "took action" and demanded a response from Him. For those who couldn't take action, Jesus responded to friends and family members who did so on their behalf.

The call of God may not be a sudden "word" from heaven to your heart. For most people, it is a gradual drawing towards a place or position.

3. The Call Is a Holy Calling

In verse 5, it says, "*'Do not come any closer,' God said. 'Take off your sandals, for the place where you are standing is holy ground.'*"

God is a holy God, and His call for us is holy. We need to respond and live in an appropriate way.

"Take off your shoes, you are standing on holy ground" is a command of God which causes us to walk differently, talk differently and live differently.

For most of us, when we became Christians, we had a strong sense of right and wrong. We knew what pleased and what didn't please God. But as we live life, our senses can often get dulled so that things that we used to find offensive no longer affect us, and things that we used to be intolerant of, we now put up with. We don't mean for our hearts to get dirty and hard, but everything we see, say, hear and do is registered in our hearts slowly over time. Our hearts get hard and we no longer feel the thorns of sin prodding us. We just tolerate and accept it.

God's statement to "Take of your shoes because you are on holy ground" is made in recognition of our need to walk differently. Take your shoes off, walk on the road and feel every stone jabbing at your foot. Equally, walk bare footed, with spiritually "soft feet", so that every sin and temptation will be a shock to your system. You'll no longer put up with sin; you'll stay clear of it, because God is holy and His plan for your life is holy.

4. The Call Is Commissioning

The word "commission" can be defined as "sent out to do a task".

In Acts 1:8 we read Jesus saying, *"But you will receive power when the Holy Spirit comes on you; and you will be my witnesses in Jerusalem, and in all Judea and Samaria, and to the ends of the earth."*

In Acts 2:1–4, we read,

> *"When the day of Pentecost came, they were all together in one place. Suddenly a sound like the*

> *blowing of a violent wind came from heaven and filled the whole house where they were sitting. They saw what seemed to be tongues of fire that separated and came to rest on each of them. All of them were filled with the Holy Spirit and began to speak in other tongues as the Spirit enabled them."*

The incident that took place between God and me in that prayer meeting when I was 12 years old was not really about me. It was about God stirring me up to tell others about Him.

There is a story which best summarises why, when God calls you, He commissions you:

Imagine the scene: Jesus has just died, been resurrected and appeared to many people over a 40-day period. Then He ascends into heaven (see Acts 1:4–9). When He arrives in heaven, the angels flock over to celebrate the actions of the Saviour of the world. They marvel at His courage, speak excitedly of His victory over Satan and whisper in hushed tones their amazement about His great love which led to such sacrifice. While this is going on, Jesus notices one of the smaller angels talking with the Archangel and so Jesus asks, "What's up?" The Archangel replies, "Master, we watched in awe as You accomplished such a great victory on behalf of humanity. Your victory was full and complete in every way, and yet we noticed that you left this good news in the hands of just a few dozen people. Some of them are impetuous, others are doubters and some of the others ... well, can they really be trusted? Surely there has to be some other way that people can hear about what You did, rather than leaving it with those people to tell others?" At this point Jesus answers and says, "I have no other way."[1]

God's plans for you may include you being a doctor, a teacher or a businessman. But in reality, you are in disguise. The reality is that you have been commissioned by God to tell others how amazing He is, but not just in words. St Francis of Assissi said,

> **"Preach the gospel at all times.**
> **Use words if necessary."**

... now, there's a challenge.

Your Summary

Write your thoughts about this chapter here and what you feel "God's call" is for your life. If you don't know what that is, set aside time to spend with God, seeking His plans and purposes for you.

Note

1. Author unknown.

Step #6

Revolutionaries "Live Fixed"

In James 5:17 it says, *"Elijah was a man just like us . . . "* You can read the story of Elijah and his friends in 1 Kings chapters 17–19 and 2 Kings chapter 2.

Elijah was the type of man you would definitely want to hang around with if you had the opportunity. Elijah could change weather patterns and part great seas.

When we read the story of Elijah in 1 Kings, we notice that evil kings had been ruling for 65 years. There were seven kings in total over that time, and King Asa was the most evil of them all. Elijah walks into the scene in an evil time.

The great showdown for Elijah came in 1 Kings chapter 18. He challenged the "false prophets" (the cult leaders) to a duel to see whose god was truly THE GOD. The rules for the battle were pretty simple. The 850 false prophets were to build an altar and place a bull on it. Elijah would do the same. Then, both the false prophets and Elijah would call down fire on their altars and the god who answered by fire would be proven to be THE GOD.

As it turns out, the god of the false prophets did not answer. Elijah even taunted them saying,

> *"Shout louder! . . . Surely he is a god! Perhaps he is deep in thought, or busy, or travelling. Maybe he is sleeping and must be awakened."*
>
> (1 Kings 18:27)

Then Elijah prayed his prayer:

> *"O LORD, God of Abraham, Isaac and Israel, let it be known today that you are God in Israel and that I am your servant and have done all these things at your command. Answer me, O LORD, answer me, so these people will know that you, O LORD, are God, and that you are turning their hearts back again."*
>
> (1 Kings 18:36–37)

God responded phenomenally:

> *"Then the fire of the LORD fell and burned up the sacrifice, the wood, the stones and the soil, and also licked up the water in the trench. When all the people saw this, they fell prostrate and cried, 'The LORD – he is God! The LORD – he is God!'"*
>
> (1 Kings 18:38–39)

Prior to God's response, Elijah had challenged the people. They had been living a "split spirituality". They had been worshippers of God one day, but then they changed and followed the false prophet's gods. Elijah refused to put up with this and said to them, *"How long will you waver between two opinions? If the LORD is God, follow him; but if Baal is God, follow him"* (verse 21). The people had thought they were strong by worshipping both gods. They felt as though they were "hedging their bets", getting the "best out of both worlds". The word "waver" literally means to "be crippled". So instead of the people being made strong by their "split spirituality" they were actually making themselves weak and vulnerable.

The challenge from Elijah was to "LIVE FIXED". If God is God, then "Live Fixed". In other words: "unwavering, solid, without looking to the left or right, without regret, with great conviction, determined and unashamed."

There are four reasons why revolutionaries need to live fixed. Take a few minutes and read Daniel 3:1–30.

1. Revolutionaries Live Fixed Because of Distraction

Verses 1–4 say,

> *"King Nebuchadnezzar made an image of gold, ninety feet high and nine feet wide, and set it up on the plain in Dura in the province of Babylon. He then summoned the satraps, prefects, governors, advisors, treasurers, judges, magistrates and all the other provincial officials to come to the dedication of the image he had set up. So* [they] *assembled for the dedication of the image ... and they stood before it. Then the herald loudly*

> *proclaimed . . . 'As soon as you hear* [the instruments] *you must fall down and worship the image of gold . . .' "*

Notice that the king didn't set up the statue in a cave, a hole or a gully. The Bible says he put it on the plain. This meant that it was in full view of everyone. People living on the hill would open their curtains in the morning and see the statue. Everyone living on the plain could see the statue rising above the rooftops. They couldn't avoid the fact that the statue was there because wherever they went, they could see it. Not only was it big, but it was also made of gold. Imagine the reflection of the sun on it. It would have been a spectacular sight.

Why was it so big? Because it was there to be *a big* distraction. Why was it so spectacular? Because it was there to be *a really big effective* distraction.

Shadrach, Meshach and Abednego are the heroes of this story. These three young men loved God, but could easily have been distracted by all that was going on around them.

The king was so adamant that *all* the people would worship the statue that he issued a decree, "*Whoever does not fall down and worship will immediately be thrown into the fiery furnace*" (verse 6). The pressure was on the three friends to be distracted from their destiny of honouring God. Their distraction could have taken place in different forms:

- A spectacular sight (the statue was big and bright)
- Conformity (all the people were worshipping it)

- The loud declaration (what voice were they listening to?)
- The music (the best musicians and bands were playing)
- The king's threat ("I'll kill you if you don't worship me.")

They had every reason to be distracted from pursuing God and yet they said these words in Daniel 3:16–18:

> *"O Nebuchadnezzar, we do not need to defend ourselves before you in this matter. If we are thrown into the blazing furnace, the God we serve is able to save us from it, and he will rescue us from your hand, O king. But even if he does not, we want you to know, O king, that we will not serve your gods or worship the image of gold you have set up."*

They saw the statue for what it really was: "an empty monument that when worshipped, would only cause their lives to crash and burn." Shadrach, Meschach and Abednego refused to get sucked in by the hype.

The dictionary defines the word "hype" as "an empty reality". Hype is when something looks and sounds fantastic, but doesn't live up to expectations.

▶ Hype is spending £44 on a console game that had rave reviews and amazing graphics (on the TV ad), only to discover it's worse than the game you invented on your computer when you were three and a half years old.

- Hype is shooting for the moon, only to get as high as Blackpool Tower.
- Hype is seeing the girl of your dreams from a distance, but noticing her whiskers close up.
- Hype is building a statue and getting everyone to worship it, when it's just a lump of metal.[1]

Revolutionaries make a choice not to fall for the hype of what the world says is worth living and giving your life for, no matter how glamorous it sounds. It will always lead away from the stuff that really counts and is of real value in life.

Society is constantly setting things up in plain view of us, in an attempt to take our attention off what is important and focus on the meaningless (i.e. image, fashion and material possessions). It distracts us from the destiny and purpose God has planned for each of us. Unless you "Live Fixed" on God and His exciting purposes for your life, you'll live distracted.

2. Revolutionaries Understand That There Is a Lot of Noise Out There

Daniel 3:4–5 says:

> *"Then the herald loudly proclaimed, 'This is what you are commanded to do, O peoples, nations and men of every language: As soon as you hear the*

> *sound of the horn, flute, zither, lyre, harp, pipes and all kinds of music, you must fall down and worship the image of gold that King Nebuchadnezzar has set up.'"*

There was "loud proclamation" (verse 4). Not only did the statue catch people's attention, but loud shouts attracted people too.

There's a lot of noise in your world right now. There are many and varied things which are trying to speak into your life: some good and some bad. There are:

- Do's and don'ts
- Expectations from family, friends and even yourself
- Pressures from everyday life situations and major moments
- Worries which come from the "What if?" syndrome

... and they are all very loud.

But there comes a time when we have to realise that enough is enough.

A few years ago at the "Audacious" conference, as I was walking around the site, I began to listen to the voice that was the loudest in my head. It was shouting, "What if the Audacious delegates don't like it? What if next year there are fewer than this year? What if ... what if ... what if ... ?" After a few days of this torture which was deeming me inept, I had to say "enough". How did I beat those voices? Audacious shouted louder. That night in the conference we were talking about the Praises of God in our mouths. I brought up one of the sound engineers with a decibel counter and the 800 delegates that year began to shout the praises of God. Those voices that had been so loud in my head just a moment earlier were drowned out by a new sound.

- If the world yells one thing – revolutionaries make more noise,
- If the pressures are on us – revolutionaries shout louder,
- The more society shouts – the more revolutionaries turn up the worship,
- The more they pressure – the more revolutionaries LIVE FIXED on the King.

3. Revolutionaries Know That Someone's Picked a Fight

Daniel 3:6 says,

> *"Whoever does not fall down and worship will immediately be thrown into a blazing furnace."*

That sounds like a challenge. Basically the challenge was:

- "If you don't do this – you're in trouble . . ."

or alternatively:

- "If don't become like us – you're busted!"

You are constantly being issued with challenges when you LIVE for God.

- In college, there will be challenges on your morality.
- In work there will be challenges on your integrity.
- In life there will be challenges to your belief system.

The truth is, "How you respond to challenges reveals what you really believe, because what you do comes out of your belief system."

Revolutionaries realise that someone's picking a fight. There are people who are bent on taking you away from the purposes of God for your life. It's a battle, a fight, and the best way to fight is to go on the offensive. Not to shy away but to stand up.

In the epic movie *Braveheart*, William Wallace puts it this way when a peaceful solution is about to be offered, "I'm off to pick a fight." Instead of lying down saying, "C'mon, hit me baby one more time," we make a decision to go on the offensive. How do we do that? Do we throw punches or become arrogant? No, we simply "LIVE FIXED". That always catches people off guard.

In verse 17, Nebuchadnezzar and his men thought that the challenge issued would make Shadrach, Meshach and Abednego tremble with fear, resulting in them doing that which was decreed. But instead of taking it lying down, they went on the offensive. They said,

- "Even if God doesn't come through – we will live fixed."

They started to fight. They were revolutionaries.

4. Revolutionaries Know That God Loves Getting His Hands Dirty

Verses 24–25 say,

> *"Then King Nebuchadnezzar leaped to his feet in amazement and asked his advisers, 'Weren't there three men that we tied up and threw into the fire?' They replied, 'Certainly, O king.' He said, 'Look. I see four men walking around in the fire, unbound and unharmed, and the fourth looks like a son of the gods.' "*

What a great image this must have been. Nebuchadnezzar must have been completely baffled by the fact that there were four people in the furnace. Imagine him calling over his most trusted advisors, saying, "Help me count … 1 … 2 … 3 … 4! Why are there four? Did any of the soldiers fall in? No? 1 … 2

. . . 3 . . . 4. I don't know who the fourth guy is, but he looks like GOD!"

God could have saved Shadrach, Meshack and Abednego before going into the furnace and He could have saved Daniel from the lions' den before he was thrown into it in chapter 6, but He didn't. Why?

Because God's plan was not to save them FROM it, His plan was to save them IN it.

When you are in "Living Fixed" territory, God meets you there. He is not a God who remains far off. He loves to get His hands dirty, to get in the ring with you.

Where previously you felt bound (verse 25), you now find yourself walking free because God came into the situation. Sometimes your situation may not change, but you'll change. That's all you need, because then, YOUR PERSPECTIVE about the situation will change. And when your perspective changes, sooner or later, you'll find the situation will also.

The most famous chapter in the Bible is Psalm 23. Look at what it says in verse 5, *"You prepare a table for me in the presence of my enemies."* Imagine the picture: you are facing an approaching army that outnumbers you 10,000 to 1. Just as they are about to attack, God says, "STOP! It's dinner time for you" and he feeds you a great meal and defeats the enemy for you. In the midst of thickest battle, the most difficult situation you have ever been in, God waits on you.

If you are having a tough time now, God is waiting

on you. Why not take some time now to talk with Him, to see what words of wisdom and encouragement He has for you from the Bible, a sermon or even your quiet time, to keep you going another day, week, month, year, or for the rest of your life.

The book of Daniel teaches that your "persecution is really your promotion." In verse 28–29 it says,

> *"Then Nebuchadnezzar said, 'Praise be to the God of Shadrach, Meshach and Abednego, who has sent his angel and rescued his servants!*
> *They trusted in him and defied the king's command and were willing to give up their lives rather than serve or worship any god except their own God.*
> *Therefore I decree that the people of any nation or language who say anything against the God of Shadrach, Meshach and Abednego be cut into pieces and their houses be turned into piles of rubble, for no other god can save in this way.' "*

When Revolutionaries "Live Fixed" for God, nations will say about us:

- "Praise be to the God of the Audacious Revolution. They trusted in Him and defied the king's command (society's wishes to confine Christians to mediocrity – anything but the audacious lifestyle) and were willing to give up their lives rather than serve or worship any God but their own ... "

Imagine that in the newspapers!!!

Your Summary

Write your thoughts about this chapter here and what you need to do to "Live Fixed".

Notes

1. Glyn Barrett, *If I Was the Devil*, Sovereign World, p. 69.

Step #7

Revolutionaries Understand Honour

Honour

hon·our: (ŏn'ər)
[*n. and v. chiefly British*]

Meaning:

- ***a tangible symbol signifying approval or distinction***
- ***an award for bravery***
- ***having a good name***
- ***to bestow rewards upon***
- ***to show respect towards***

n. 1: the state of being honoured [syn. honour, laurels] [ant. dishonour] 2: a tangible symbol signifying approval or distinction; an award for bravery [syn. award, accolade, honour, laurels] 3: the quality of being honourable and having a good name: "a man of honour" [syn. honour] [ant. dishonour] 4: a woman's virtue or chastity [syn. honour, purity] v. 1: bestow honour or rewards upon: "Today we honour our soldiers"; "The scout was rewarded for courageous action" [syn. honour, reward] [ant. dishonour] 2: show respect towards: "honour your parents." [syn. respect, honour, abide by, observe] [ant: disrespect] 3: accept as pay; "we honour cheques and drafts" [syn. honour] [ant. dishonour] [1]

Honour is a word that is not frequently used or demonstrated in the youth generation, and yet the generation that honours is a generation that will accomplish what others have only ever dreamed of accomplishing.

There is a massive place for "honour" in society today. A simple read of national and local newspapers reveals a complete lack of honour for national leaders. The Prime Minister and monarchy are regularly and habitually maligned, abused, and scrutinized in some appalling ways. It is so bad at times, that it actually becomes a bit of a game to find something positive to say about the leaders of the nation. The lack of honour is so bad, that it would be a great occasion if the Prime Minister meets some Audacious revolutionaries who understood and displayed honour.

There are two things, amongst several, that are really worth honouring:

1. The Word of God

Audacious revolutionaries realise that the Word of God is the most awesome book available. It is the best selling book worldwide – ever. The reason? Because it's God's thoughts, direct from heaven, right into the hearts of those who want to hear from Him.

Revolutionaries know that men and woman have died for the cause of making the Bible available for us today. They know that blood has been spilled so we can read and preach from the Word of God. They see the point in prayerfully reading the pages of the book and asking questions of the words they read like, "Why did the apostle Paul write those words? Why didn't Jesus heal everyone He saw? Why does Matthew chapter 1 give a long list of the generations? And what caused King David to sin so dreadfully with Bathsheba?"

Revolutionaries know that the Bible is a love letter from the heart of God to those He loves. The Audacious generation know that the pages of the book are crammed full with knowledge and tips on how to live "most excellent lives" and so they read it. They see the power of God at work in the pages of the Bible and are inspired to live it out today, asking the question, "If it can happen in the book of Acts, then why can't it happen now?" And so they read it.

Revolutionaries realise that the Book of Acts is the only book of the Bible which has no logical or grammatical ending, because that book is still being written by young people who rise with an Audacious spirit to attempt and achieve great things for God.

Above all, Audacious revolutionaries understand five distinct things about the Word of God.

(i) The Word creates POWER

Jeremiah 20:9 says,

> *"But if I say, 'I will not mention him*
> *or speak anymore in his name,'*
> *his word is in my heart like a fire,*
> *a fire shut up in my bones.*
> *I am weary of holding it in;*
> *indeed, I cannot."*

Jeremiah couldn't help but speak about God because he was ON FIRE.

Car engines prove that "power comes from fire". The spark plugs in the car create a SPARK (fire) and that spark in turn creates energy which is turned into acceleration and momentum for that car – POWER is created!

For Jeremiah, the Word of God was like a fire that created a power source within him, which led him to be able to affect a nation. Revolutionaries ask, "How can one youth ministry impact a nation?" The answer comes down to you as an individual. If you haven't got the Word like a FIRE in your spirit, then you haven't got any POWER. If your friends in youth haven't got the Word like a fire, then they have no power either, and if the whole youth ministry hasn't got the Word of God like a fire, there is no power to affect a locality let alone a nation.

But what happens if you and your mate HAVE got the Word like fire? Then you are on your way to building a powerful band of revolutionaries who in turn will affect the world around them.

(ii) The Word makes something happen

Genesis 1:1 says, *"In the beginning God . . . "* and then in verses 3, 6, 9 and 11 it says, *"And God said . . . and there was . . . "*

Whenever God speaks, something always happens. Heaven and earth turn to look and Satan begins to tremble. All because "GOD SAID".

In verse 2 in the NKJV it says that the earth was, *". . . without form, and void . . . "* Void simply means "nothing there". So there was nothing, but when "God said", something happened. God's Word always does that. Whenever your spirit feels dry or you feel like there is nothing going on in your life, the best thing you can do is spend time in the Word of God. Because in the middle of your "void" God can speak and make something happen in your life.

God is amazing, because He needs NOTHING in order to make SOMETHING. Our greatest scientists need to start with *something* in order to create something else. Someone once described it this way:

> Some clever scientists once approached God and said, "Anything you can do, we can do. We challenge you to a duel, God. We challenge you to make a human being. We have learnt the art of cloning humans and we are convinced we can do better that you." To which God replied, "I accept the challenge on one condition. The condition is

> that you have to create a human from what I used back in the beginning with Adam. You have to use *dust*" (see Genesis 2:7). The scientists agreed and bent to pick up some dust, at which point God shouted, "Hey, get your own dust!"

God needed nothing back in the beginning. There was a void, but God made something happen. If you feel a little bit void at the moment, then all you need is the Word of God and to watch – something will begin to happen!

(iii) The Word directs

Psalm 119:105 says,

> *"Your word is a lamp to my feet*
> *and a light for my path."*

We all get frustrated with God. He speaks to us about areas of life and ministry, but we want to see all that He has in store for us. The trouble is that He often just shows us some and not *all* of it.

The Bible says, "The Word of God is a light". If the Word is a light, then why can't we see very far into what God has for us? Why can't we see what next year, the next ten years, the next thirty years have for us?

The answer is simple. When it comes to the Word of God for our lives, God requires us to step out in faith in the areas He has spoken to us about, understanding that the more we walk, the more we will see.

Audacious Revolutionaries don't wait for the full picture. Once God speaks, Revolutionaries get up and start walking in that light.

(iv) The Word gives you something to eat

Matthew 4:4 says,

> *"Jesus answered, 'It is written: "Man does not live on bread alone, but on every word that comes from the mouth of God."' "*

We live in a world of fast cars, fast work, and fast food. We have take away, delivery, chip and pin, internet shopping and banking, and we love it. We love it because it's quick, easy, fast and efficient.

Sometimes we fall into the trap of thinking God is slow. In reality, God invented quick, easy, fast and efficient. He actually created the universe in six days.

Because we're into fast and efficient, we can begin to treat the Word of God like a "Drive Thru" food experience. We can develop lifestyles that say, "God, I haven't got time for the Word this week so, I'll go to church on Sunday and grab something at the Drive Thru." Somehow, church has become a fast-food restaurant and the sermon is the Drive Thru section.

As God is always nice, He gives us some great nuggets to chew on for the following week from the sermon that was just preached. He meets us at another meeting and we get a quick Drive Thru service.

Take away food is good in small doses, but home cooking is the absolute best. Revolutionaries learn to "home cook" the Word. You don't need another sermon; you need to start cooking yourself. Sunday and Wednesday in church is just dessert. Dessert is nice – but you can't live on it.

Sunday sermon Christians are no different from those of "other" religions who need a priest to find God. The Bible says that you don't need a priest because Jesus became the "Great High Priest" for you. As revolutionaries know, you can get the Word of God out for yourself and listen to God on your own.

(v) The Word compels

In 1 Corinthians 9:16 it says,

> *"Yet when I preach the gospel, I cannot boast, for I am compelled to preach. Woe to me if I do not preach the gospel."*

The dictionary defines "compel" as an "irresistible urge". The Word of God is something that gives you "irresistible urges".

When you read and "eat" the Bible, you can't help but:

- live full on for God
- make right choices
- have fun
- live for the purposes of God
- win your world
- make disciples
- do great things
- go the extra mile.

If the Word doesn't compel you, then something else will. So what compels you the most in life? Is it sin? Is it circumstances around you? Is it people's words? Or is it God's words?

One of the definitions of honour was,

- a tangible symbol signifying approval or distinction

Revolutionaries honour the Word of God by becoming the tangible symbol that signifies that they read and believe the Word of God to be the most dynamic force at work in their lives. They approve of it and live it out. Revolutionaries honour God by reading and living the Word of God in action.

2. Leaders

The second key thing that revolutionaries honour is their leaders. The Bible says that, "God raises leaders and sets them in place." To dishonour leadership is, in effect, to dishonour God.

Honour can be defined as:

- "showing respect towards"

Some people don't honour leaders because they don't agree with what the leader has said or done. But honour is not about agreement (although that is very important). It is about showing respect.

Respect is when you maintain a good heart and attitude towards someone else. It is when you put the wishes of that person above those of your own, refusing to only ever do things when it is in your own best interest.

Honour is shown by thanking leaders for the work they do, not pointing out where they should do better. Honour is displayed by thinking through ways of "blessing" the leader, thereby enabling them to feel encouraged. Honour is revealed by living out the biblical principle of "servanthood".

In Mark 10:43–45 Jesus says,

> *"Not so with you. Instead, whoever wants to become great among you must be your servant, and whoever wants to be first must be slave of all. For even the Son of Man did not come to be served, but to serve, and to give his life as a ransom for many."*

The term "servant" conjures up images of people who are downtrodden and used. Not many careers teachers would encourage their students to follow servanthood as a vocation, as it doesn't carry a great reputation. In the Bible, however, we are presented with a completely different image of what it means to honour through servanthood.

The word "servant" is translated from seven different terms in the New Testament, which was originally written in Greek. These seven different aspects give us a better understanding of honouring through servanthood:

(i) Doulos

Doulos means "bound to God". When we become Christians, we exchange our bondage to "sin" for being bound to God. To be a servant in the Bible means to live a life that is devoted to God. He saved us from the power and penalty of sin. He rescued us from a horrible eternity. All we could offer Him was sin, pain and hurt. In exchange God offered us a "full life" (John 10:10).

(ii) Pais

Pais means "children". Sometimes in our attempt to be "mature" we lose our "childlike" faith. When I come home from work, my two children run to the top of the stairs in our house and jump at me. It wouldn't be so bad if there were only three steps. There are fourteen. When they jump, they don't doubt whether daddy will catch them. I clamber up the stairs and catch them. Sometimes we complicate our Christianity too much. We should be more childlike. My Youth Pastor once said, "Love God – hate sin." That sounds pretty simple ... yet, profound too.

(iii) Oiletes

Oiletes means, "house servant". Another name for church is the "House of God". When you honour your leaders in church life by serving on the teams they ask you to be a part of, you become a "house servant". Those who work on behalf of others in the house make it a better place. They make it more attractive for visitors who think church is out of date and irrelevant. The "house servant" works to change that mindset.

(iv) Sun Doulos

Sun doulos means "Fellow servant". It means that you understand that church is part of the family of God and when you serve, you serve with others who are equally "sold out" to see church become everything it should be. There is a sense that "we're in this together". As we serve, we serve together to make God known in our towns and cities.

(v) Therapin

Therapin means "to heal". The English word "therapy" is a derivative of this word. It is an amazing truth in the Bible. It literally tells us that as we honour through serving we "heal" ourselves. Many people who are hurt, distressed or lonely, or carrying depression or bitterness, can be healed through simply serving. The effect of taking your eyes off yourself to help others has the amazing effect of making your own problems feel small. In fact, many problems fade into insignificance when you realise that life is not just about you. It's about those who you do life with. In fact as you serve, you also help to heal other people from their insecurities and problems.

(vi) Diakonos

The word *diakonos* simply means "to serve". In Acts 6:1–7, we read about "men" who were recognised to be full of the Holy Spirit. They were asked to "wait" on tables – in other words, to serve the church in practical ways so that others in turn could do the jobs of "preaching, praying, evangelism . . . "

(vii) Huperetes

The final definition is the word *huperetes* which simply means "minister/officer". Ministers in church life are also servants.

Your Summary

Write your thoughts about this chapter here and what you need to do to in order to honour the Word of God and your leaders.

Notes

1. www.dictionary.com.

Step #8

Revolutionaries Are Enthusiastic

Enthusiasm

enthusiasm: (ĕn-tho͞o'zē-ăz'əm)
[*Late Latin enthūsiasmus, from Greek enthousiasmos, from enthousiazein, to be inspired by God, from entheos, possessed: en-, in; see* ***en-*** *+ theos, God; see dhēs- in Indo-European Roots.*]

Meaning:

- ***to rave***
- ***to go into raptures***
- ***to go overboard***

Somehow the church has got the reputation of being boring and tedious. Somehow the church has presumed that reverence and holiness are akin to melancholic worship and monosyllabic monologues presented by men who are equally melancholic and unenthused.

And yet the very word "enthusiasm" stems from the Greek word *entheos* meaning "in God". If anything, the church should have the monopoly on enthusiasm, because the reality is that it comes from the state of being "in God".

When you have a revelation of what God did for you by dying on the cross, and you understand the magnitude of what it cost Him to rescue you – you can't help but be enthusiastic.

The option of "raving, going into raptures and going overboard" no longer remains simply a choice for us: it is something we do out of necessity, in response to what God has done for us.

Revolutionaries know that. That is why they get accused of "going a little bit too far in worship". That is why they are asked to calm down their boisterous style of praise and worship and to be a little quieter in response to the preached word. But revolutionaries can't help it. They are loud. They are proud to be loud, because they realise that while the world is loud about a lot of other things, there is something in salvation worth making even more noise about.

Recently in a church service, a critic of the boisterous style of worship took great delight in saying, "*These people* are jumping around like idiots." The response to that man came back loud and clear. "Do you see that 16-year-old boy jumping up and down in worship? He was going nowhere fast. He had no friends and was hooked on drugs, but God got hold of his life and he is now free of drugs and has loads of friends in church. He also has a purpose and destiny to live for." "Do you see that married couple with their hands raised in worship? Before they became Christians they were involved in extra-marital affairs.

They were on the brink of divorce and it looked likely that a fierce custody battle would take place over who got the rights to keep the children. But God got hold of them. They now love each other more than ever and their kids love coming to church to worship God."

"Do you see that young woman over there? She was abused by an uncle when she was young and carried hurt and bitterness and a complete inability to love anyone because of her pain. But God got a hold of her – everything is different now."

The response to that critic became even more pointed. "So, who are you, saying that these people are jumping around like idiots? They are enthusiastic and passionate in worship because their God is not just a figment of their imagination. He is not a stained glass window or a far distant deity. He is real. He has picked them up, He has healed their hurts and they can't help but respond to God in a way that is full of passion and enthusiasm."

It was a good answer to a man who knew about "God – the theory" but had no understanding of "God – the Father". When you know God as your Father, it speaks of your relationship with Him – a relationship that begins when He first grabs your attention and you say "Yes" in response to His great love for you. That response then leads you to change the way you are living, to begin to live with the ethos, "Jesus, if You could die for me, then the least I can do is live for You." Revolutionaries know that Jesus died "enthusiastically" (enthusiasm means "to go overboard"). Surely Jesus went overboard when He died for the sins of mankind. He could have come to earth at a time when the form of death inflicted by man was quick and relatively pain-free. But He didn't. He came to earth at a time when crucifixion was the method of assassination. Death wasn't quick, easy, or pain free. It was overboard. Revolutionaries understand that. That is why they, in turn, live enthusiastic lives for God. "If You could die for me, then the least I can do is live for You."

In Acts 3:1–10, there is an amazing account of a man responding to God. There are five lessons that revolutionaries can learn about Enthusiasm from this passage.

1. Enthusiasm Is for Church on Sunday

In verse 8 we read how the man responds to God as a result of his healing:

> *"He jumped to his feet and began to walk. Then he went with them into the temple courts, walking and jumping, and praising God."*

The first thing he does in his enthusiasm is that he takes it into church. Notice that, "*. . . he went with them into the temple courts . . .*"

One of the greatest hypocrisies within Christianity today has to be the Christian who jumps around like crazy at a football game or in response to some good news at work, but sits sullenly in church on a Sunday, and rarely breaks into a smile. Somehow, the church has become the holding station for "all things dull and horrible". Many people in society today choose not to go to church on Sunday because the very mention of the word CHURCH is enough to bring to mind images of irrelevance, tedium and the smell of mothballs. But in this passage in Acts, enthusiasm went first into church.

Back when Buddy Holly first played Rock 'n' Roll on a café roof in the USA, the church had an opportunity to bring "enthusiasm" back into church worship and culture. Buddy, the son of a minister, was not looked on so kindly by those in the church, and so he went to other venues where there was not just tolerance but an overwhelming acceptance of this new style of music.

Imagine what would have happened if the church had realised that it is where enthusiasm should appear first, and from there flow into society. If the church had taken on board this new music revolution, then perhaps MTV and other music stations wouldn't be so "X-rated". Perhaps there would even be a mainstream acceptance of "Christian" music in the music industry today. Perhaps the church would be the "movers and shakers" in the culture of music, rather than having Christian bands likened to secular bands so that you can understand the "style" of band they truly are ... imagine the day when new secular bands are likened in style to Christian bands who are fast setting the pace in an all-new music revolution. Could it happen? Perhaps if the church got a little more enthusiastic about "doing church"?!

Revolutionaries are aware of this. That's why their worship is so loud and passionate. That is why a focus on excellence is taught to musicians and singers in the

"Audacious" style of worship. In fact, Revolutionaries know that when they play and sing in worship bands and groups, they are in fact "performers". They are performing outwardly everything God has done on the inside of them.

2. Enthusiasm Catches Up with the Face and the Body

Verse 8 says that he went into church *"walking and jumping"*.

There are many Christians who don't smile much, or show much "enthusiasm" in their worship or even their Christian lifestyle. The comment may often be heard, "I am enthusiastic on the inside." If ever a lie was told, that is one! The reality about enthusiasm is that it catches up with your face and your body.

Picture a British game of football. The fans of opposing teams are always segregated due to their "passion" which is often displayed as aggression, and which invariably results in fighting. Hence the segregation. There will always be occasions when you are desperate to see your team play, but you are unable to get tickets to sit with the rest of "your fans". What do you do? You buy a ticket to sit with the other supporters and tell yourself not to cheer when your team scores a goal. What happens when your team scores? Invariably you forget your plan, stand to your feet and cheer – usually regretting that outward display of enthusiasm as you are escorted from the stadium for your own protection.

Picture school: you are in class, and the teacher is the meanest in the whole school. You are not allowed to mess about in class because your teacher is liable to "eat you" or some other ghastly thing. So what happens when your friend says something funny and you get the giggles? The more you try to suppress the laughter, the more it flows until you can't help yourself and you laugh audibly.

In Acts 3, the man is happy and enthusiastic on the inside and it shows on his face and on his movements. Enthusiasm has a habit of "not staying put". It is like torrential rain on a rickety roof. The water always manages to find a way of leaking through the roof and into the building. The point is simple: if you are happy on the inside, your face and body reflect it. Enthusiastic church worship is not displayed by solemn faces. There are times to be solemn, but there should always be times of "overboard praise and worship".

3. Enthusiasm Is the True Response of a Worshipper

Verse 9 says, *"When all the people saw him walking and praising God . . . "* His walking and jumping were evidence to all the bystanders that he was praising God. There was something right and good about the man's response to what God had done. There was no debate from the religious onlookers who were questioning his right to dance. There was no deacon asking the "revolutionary" to be a little bit quieter. Not even the temple priest challenged the man or asked him to stand solemnly so he could give a "proper" response to God. His jumping and leaping and walking were fitting for the occasion. The man had just been healed of an inability to walk. Nothing was going to stop him from showing his praise to God with everything that was within him.

Revolutionaries have an understanding that "they too" are like that healed man. God has taken revolutionaries who were "dead in their trespasses and sin" (Ephesians 2:1) and made them "alive to Christ" (Ephesians 2:5). Nothing will stop them from being enthusiastic in praise to their God. They realise that they were headed to a Christ-less eternity. They know that they had no purpose, hope or peace without God. They know that they are indebted to their God and so they dance, and they jump, and they shout, and they audibly "agree" with the preaching of the Word on a Sunday, and they can't sit still because God has "saved them".

4. Enthusiasm Is a Recipe for Trouble

One of the consequences of enthusiasm is that it has a habit of creating trouble. In Acts 4:3, Peter and John are placed in jail as a result of the man's healing and his subsequent outburst of enthusiasm. Peter is compelled to preach about what happened to the man. If the man had said a quiet "Thank you" to Peter and John and walked off into the sunset, then Peter would never have been compelled to preach. And he would never have been placed in jail. But, enthusiasm caused trouble for Peter and John. Enthusiasm always does.

But then again, Revolutionaries don't mind causing trouble ... it's what Revolutionaries do.

5. Enthusiasm Is Evangelism

In Acts 3:10–11 it says,

> *"They recognized him as the same man who used to sit begging at the temple gate called Beautiful, and they were filled with wonder and amazement at what had happened to him. While the beggar held on to Peter and John, all the people were astonished and came running to them in the place called Solomon's Colonnade."*

In Acts 4:4, it says,

> *". . . many who heard the message believed, and the number of men grew to about five thousand."*

The man's healing and enthusiastic response to God caused people to sit up and take notice. It made people ask different questions from the ones they had previously been asking about church.

In society today people make presumptions about church based on historic evidence. They ask questions like, "Why does it have to be so boring? Why do I have to go to another baptism? Do I have to go to church for Christmas again?"

When they see the enthusiasm of Revolutionaries, the questions asked about church and Christians change. People begin to ask, "What's going on there? Why are you smiling so much? Why is everyone jumping around? Why does the sermon make sense? Why is everyone so friendly? Is this place for real?"

And then their questions progress into statements like, "I have to get some of that", "Can God do the same for me too?" and "If He can do it for you, He can do it for me", "I need to know your God."

In Acts 3:11, it says that people came *"running"* to church. It poses the question, "When did people last run to your church service?" Revolutionaries live enthusiastic passionate lives because "Evangelistic potency" intensifies when people who don't know God see you living like you believe what you say you believe.

Your Summary

Write your thoughts about this chapter here and what you need to do to in order to become more enthusiastic. Which areas do you need to be more enthusiastic in?

Step #9

Revolutionaries Have the "Lion Spirit"

Proverbs 28:1 says,

> *"The wicked man flees though no-one pursues,*
> *but the righteous are as bold as a lion."*

There are three types of people in this verse. The first is a person who is aimless. It says that no-one is chasing them. In other words, there is no reason for this person to be running. Most people run for a purpose. They run to get fit, they run to win or they run to escape the dog that is chasing them. But this man's run is aimless. It has no purpose; there is no destination. Many people in society today are just like that man. They are "running" through life with no clear understanding of what life is really all about, why they are living it or where they are headed.

The second person in the passage is the one who is running to escape reality. Often people do all sorts of things in order to escape reality. They use credit cards to escape the reality that they really have no money to pay for what they want. Others turn to all varieties of pleasure just to escape the reality of what is happening in their life at that current moment in time.

But the third person in the verse is the "righteous

man". "Righteous" simply means to be "in relationship with God". The characteristic of people who are in relationship with God is that they are as "Bold as the Lion".

In 1 Samuel 17:22–50 we read about the "Lion Spirit" generation. It is the story of David and Goliath and there are three key characteristics of the "Lion Spirit".

1. Fear Nothing!

Lions have no fear. They parade around in the African jungle without a care in the world. Their determination, confidence and even arrogance has led to them being labelled the "the king of the jungle".

In verses 22–26, David had no fear (or if he did, he hid it well). When all the other men were running for cover under the shadow of the giant, David was focused and determined in his pursuit to understand what would be done for the man who killed goliath. The Bible says he neither "trembled with fear" nor "shook in anguish". He simply wanted to know what he would win for taking on the champion of the enemy.

"Fear" may be defined as a thought or feeling that is based on what *might* happen:

- You might have a nasty accident ... but you might not
- You might fall over and hurt yourself ... but you might not

- You might have bad luck if you walk under a ladder ... but you might not
- You might fail your exams ... but you might not
- You might catch a cold ... but you might not
- You might lose against Goliath ... but you might not

"Faith" is also a thought or feeling based on what *might* happen:

- You might succeed in your business ... and you might as well
- You might grow your youth ministry to 100 ... and you might as well
- You might pass your exams ... and you might as well
- You might achieve all your dreams ... and you might as well
- You might beat Goliath ... and you might as well

The great difference between Fear and Faith is that Fear restricts and Faith releases. Revolutionaries rise up with the attitude that when given the choice between FEAR or FAITH, they choose faith.

Revolutionaries don't live their lives based on negative "What ifs":

- What if I have a nasty accident?
- What if I fall over and hurt myself?
- What if I have bad luck?
- What if I fail my exams?
- What if I catch a cold?
- What if I lose to Goliath?
- What if the youth ministry fails?

Revolutionaries choose to go forward on the positive "What ifs":

- What if we have stadiums full of people worshipping God?
- What if my youth ministry grows beyond all my expectations?
- What if my best friend becomes a Christian?
- What if we succeed?

**The Lion Generation FEARS NOTHING.
It doesn't even fear failure.**

In verse 40 it says that David picked up five stones. Some theologians like to say it was because Goliath had four brothers. Revolutionaries know why he picked up five stones. It's because David's mentality was,

- If I fail with the first stone, at least I've got four more
- If I fail with the second stone, at least I've got three more
- If I fail with the third stone, at least I've got two more
- If I fail with the fourth stone, at least I've got one more
- If I fail with the fifth stone, at least I'll be light enough to run fast!

2. Attempt Anything!

In verse 48, David (the amateur soldier) attempted what the professional soldiers would not:

> *"As the Philistine moved closer to attack him, David ran quickly toward the battle line to meet him."*

Revolutionaries often find themselves surrounded by "professional Christians" who create pictures of things that can't be done. Things have been "tried and tested" before and they didn't work. The revolutionary knows that just because something was "tried and tested" and found not to work before, it only proves that that thing didn't work when it was last "tried and tested"! Revolutionaries want to know, "What about now?" They seek to try and test things today.

The revolutionary doesn't attempt stupid things. Faith is not stupid, it is simply responding to God. There are three key areas that revolutionaries attempt:

(i) A different way of looking at things

- When all the soldiers were saying, "Goliath is too big to kill", David was looking at it differently. His view was simply, "Goliath is too big to miss."
- Revolutionaries learn to stop concentrating on problems and become solution finders. Where many circumstances are problems to some, the

revolutionary revels in the chance to find the solution to that problem.

- The problem is not that the young people in the youth groups have no money or always have to travel long distances to get to good Christians events. The problem is that leaders focus on the problem instead of the potential outcome.

Revolutionaries understand the statement "the glass is half full", and choose to make it their motto for life and leadership.

(ii) A culture of enthusiasm

- In verse 48, it says that David RAN towards Goliath. He didn't meander towards him with a sullen expression. He "raved, went into raptures, went overboard" in his zeal to kill the enemy.

(iii) A youth ministry as big as hell's

- Every weekend in the city you live in, there is a youth/young adult ministry that is "far bigger" numerically than your churches. Young men and women queue for great lengths of time, often in the rain, ready to pay huge amounts of money to enter a club or bar. They will dance, drink and have a lot of fun. The place is not necessarily bad, but the essence of it is that most of them are living for themselves, with complete disregard for God and His values. In truth, if you are not living for heaven's values, you are living for hell's values. There is no in between. "No man's land" does not exist.

- Revolutionaries see packed clubs on Friday and Saturday nights and devote all their time and energy to seeing church jammed with even more people throughout the week because "Heaven's youth ministry" should be bigger than hell's.

David, the amateur, attempted what the professionals would not. Audacious Revolutionaries remember that professionals built the *Titanic*, but amateurs built the Ark. The Revolutionary is not a professional, just a young guy or girl willing to attempt anything.

3. Achieve Something!

Young David achieved four staggering "somethings" in his defeat of Goliath.

(i) He broke a stalemate

- The Bible says in 1 Samuel 17:16, *"For forty days the Philistine* [Goliath] *came forward every morning and evening and took his stand."* Imagine the scene. Every day, the Israelites would march out onto the battle lines. In reply, the Philistine army would march out to their battle lines. They would eyeball each other until Goliath stepped forward to issue the challenge. Perhaps the Israelites hoped that Goliath would be taken sick from one day to the next.

- This stalemate lasted for forty days. But David broke that stale mate.
- The stalemate in your youth ministry may be a lack of growth. All it takes is one Audacious young person to break the stalemate.

(ii) He brought victory to an army and nation

- In verse 52, victory is won for the Israelite nation.
- One young man stood in defiance of the situation and brought about a great victory for the nation. David was an average boy, who was forgotten (1 Samuel 16:11), rejected (1 Samuel 17:28) and intimidated (1 Samuel 17:43–44), and yet he single-handedly brought a great victory.
- In Ezekiel 22:30 God says,

> *"I looked for a man among them who would build up the wall and stand before me in the gap on behalf of the land so I would not have to destroy it, but I found none."*

God still looks for one. He doesn't need an army, or a committee. He just needs one person sold out to Him and His cause in order for great victories to be won. Audacious Revolutionaries are such people.

(iii) He made an intimidated army brave again

- 1 Samuel 17:52 says,

  "Then the men of Israel and Judah surged forward with a shout and pursued the Philistines to the entrance of Gath and to the gates of Ekron. Their dead were strewn along the Shaaraim road to Gath and Ekron."

  The army that was once intimidated rose up with new determination to overcome the enemy.

- Perhaps your church and youth group stand intimidated by the world around them. The Revolutionary doesn't wait to be led into arenas of great influence, Revolutionaries step out and lead others into their victories.

(iv) He left a legacy of giant killers

- In 1 Chronicles 20:4–8 it says,

  "In the course of time, war broke out with the Philistines, at Gezer. At that time Sibbecai the Hushathite killed Sippai, one of the descendants of the Rephaites, and the Philistines were subjugated. In another battle with the Philistines, Elhanan son of Jair killed Lahmi the brother of Goliath the Gittite, who had a spear with a shaft like a weaver's rod. In still another battle, which took place at Gath, there was a huge man with six fingers on each hand and six toes on each foot – twenty-four in all. He also was descended from

Rapha. When he taunted Israel, Jonathan son of Shimea, David's brother, killed him. These were descendants of Rapha in Gath, and they fell at the hands of David and his men."

- Not only did David kill a giant, but he created "giant killers" also.

- Revolutionaries do not achieve great things for God just for themselves. They create a new status norm for what can be achieved.

- Roger Bannister was the first man to run the mile in under four minutes. Accurate times for the mile run (1.609 km) weren't recorded until after 1850, when the first precisely measured running tracks were built. Foot racing had become popular in England by the 17th century, when footmen would race and their masters would wager on the result. By the 19th century "pedestrianism", as it was called, had become very popular.

  The best times recorded in the 19th century were by professionals. Even after professional foot racing died out, it wasn't until 1915 that the professional record of 4:12.75 set by Walter George in 1886 was beaten by an amateur. Progression of the mile record accelerated in the 1940s, as Swedes Arne Anderson and Gunder Hägg lowered the record to just over four minutes (4:01.4) before racing was curtailed due to World War II. After the war, it was John Landy of Australia and Britain's Roger Bannister who took up the challenge of being the first to break the fabled four minute mile barrier. Bannister did it first, and Landy did it 45 days later. Fifty years later the record is 3:43.13.[1]

- When Bannister broke the four minute mile on 6 May 1954, it was said that it would be impossible for a man to run a mile within four minutes. Within three years of Bannister first running the four minute mile four other runners had accomplished the same feat. He left a legacy of the "four minute - achievable - mile".
- Revolutionaries set a standard for others to follow.

One preacher famously said, "It's possible to live life and achieve nothing." Not Audacious Revolutionaries. They,

- ***fear nothing***
- ***attempt anything***
- ***achieve something***

... because they have the LION SPIRIT.

Your Summary

Write your thoughts about this chapter here and what you need to do to live out the "Lion Spirit".

Notes

1. www.absoluteastronomy.com/encyclopedia/

Step #10

Revolutionaries See Dead People

There is a generation rising in the nation and the nations of the world with an attitude that says, "It's time to create the type of church that is worth going to." The problem is not God. The problem is His image. God's got an image crisis and it's called "the church". People love the idea of a benevolent God. It's church that's the problem and Revolutionaries realise that they need to reinvent the church to connect with a world that's passing it by, waving to it on the way to a lost eternity. There is a generation with the Audacious spirit who are determined to see that the message of Jesus Christ is no longer for small buildings on back streets, but that it is for the main stage. It's time to put the gospel in the centre of our society.

In the movie *The Sixth Sense*, Bruce Willis plays a child psychologist who is called in to see a little boy by the name of Cole Sear. Cole is only eight years old, but is incredibly disturbed by all kinds of things that are happening to him. As the consultant doctor, Willis is called to treat this little boy. In one scene, the doctor is sitting by the little boy's bed while the little boy tells the doctor his secret: "I see dead people."

One of the main reasons that many Christians view evangelism as a passionless event is because they don't see unsaved people as "dead people". If the Bible is true, most of our family, friends and neighbours are "dead" (Ephesians 2:1). They live, work, go to school, look good, go on holiday; but the Bible says they are dead. Audacious Revolutionaries realise that if the gospel is as good as we say it is, it shouldn't be the passionless experience people believe it to be.

The sad plight of many church ministers is that they are often more concerned about removing chewing gum from the carpet, than people who desperately need contact with their Saviour. Many of our churches are in passionate pursuit of their own agendas, while God's heart is broken over a dead world. If we don't see people as dead people, then we'll live a passionless existence when it comes to evangelism.

Revolutionaries are consumed by dead people. In supermarkets, football matches, and concerts, revolutionaries don't just see the masses, they are consumed by "masses of dead people". These people are not zombies. The Bible says in Ephesians 2:1,

> *"As for you, you were* ***dead*** *in your transgressions and sins."*
>
> (emphasis added)

The revolutionary is aware that Jesus doesn't want just to help this generation out just a little bit. THE GOSPEL is that you were dead and now you are alive. You passed from darkness to light. You were going to hell and now you are going to heaven. The Audacious revolutionary has a theology that has so captivated their hearts that they are obsessed with dead people.

"This is a dead generation." It's trendy, designer-label focused, but still dead.

In Ezekiel 37:1–10 we read,

> *"The hand of the LORD was upon me, and he brought me out by the Spirit of the LORD and set me in the middle of a valley; it was full of bones. He led me back and forth among them, and I saw a great many bones on the floor of the valley, bones that were very dry. He asked me, 'Son of man, can these bones live?' I said, 'O Sovereign LORD, you alone know.' Then he said to me, 'Prophesy to these bones and say to them, "Dry bones, hear the word of the LORD. This is what the Sovereign LORD says to these bones: I will make breath enter you, and you will come to life. I will attach tendons to you and make flesh come upon you and cover you with skin; I will put breath in you, and you will come to life. Then you will know that I am the LORD."' So I prophesied as I was commanded. And as I was prophesying, there was a noise, a rattling sound, and the bones came together, bone to bone. I looked, and tendons and flesh appeared on them and skin covered them, but there was no breath in them. Then he said to me, 'Prophesy to the breath; prophesy, son of man, and say to it, "This is what the Sovereign LORD says: Come from the four winds, O breath, and breathe into these slain, that they may live."' So I prophesied as he commanded me, and breath entered them; they came to life and stood up on their feet – a vast army."*

There are two keys in the art of "seeing dead people".

1. Visit the "Valley of Death"

In verse 1 it says that God took Ezekiel to a valley of death. At that point, God asked Ezekiel the most ridiculous question. God has a habit of asking us questions. Not because He doesn't know the answers, but because He wants us to get engaged on His wavelength so that we will know the answers for ourselves.

God's question was simple: "Ezekiel, can these bones live?" At this point, Ezekiel finds himself in a bit of a "no-win" situation. If he says, "No," God might zap him. The really worrying thing is, if he stands in the valley and says, "Yes Lord, these bones can live" then maybe God will expect him to do something about it!

Revolutionaries want to see dead people but the implication of seeing dead people is that you, just like Ezekiel will be called upon by God to do something about it. Why you? The answer is simple, because they are dead and God has put you in that valley to do something about it. Revolutionaries are aware that their schools, universities, colleges, workplaces and neighbourhoods are in fact their valley of dry bones.

You may think, "How can my mate Joel, who's really cool but not a Christian, be dead? He's got more life than half the duffers in our church. How can Joel be dead?" The answer is found in the truth that there are three parts to your being. Firstly, your body. We've all got a body. Some are big, some are small, but everyone has a body. Secondly we've all got a soul.

Your soul is your emotions, your character and your personality. It's the thing that makes you different from the person sat next to you. Chemically you are no different from anybody else, but it's the soul that distinguishes you from everybody else. It's what makes us the kind of people we are. Thirdly, every person on the planet has a spirit. The Bible says that before you know Christ and repent of your sin, your spirit is dead. It's not just a bit dead. It's totally dead.

We are made up of body, soul and spirit. There may be people in your family with a body and with a soul, but their spirit is totally dead towards God.

The Bible encourages us not to be in relationship (courtship/marriage) with people who don't know God (2 Corinthians 6:14). Why? Answer: Why would we want to share our lives intimately with a corpse? They're walking around but there's a bit of them that is dead. They're playing football, but they are dead. They are going to concerts dead. And all too often, we don't see those dead people. We see people as doing okay; that's why evangelism has become so passionless. That's why many of our youth groups haven't grown – because we're taking people a message we don't even think they need. When you understand that the world is dead, when you see dead people, it develops something inside of you that cannot be shut up.

God took Ezekiel to a dry valley and said "Can these bones live?" God asks the same question of Revolutionaries: "Do you see dead people? Can they live?" Revolutionaries see dead people. When Jesus saw crowds, He was moved to compassion. Why? Because He saw dead people.

2. When it's Dry, Prophesy

Ezekiel 37:4 says, *"Then he said to me, 'Prophesy to these bones and say to them, "Dry bones, hear the word of the LORD!"' "*

Truly prophetic people are fed up with the "I'll wait and see" crowd (meaning, we'll wait and see if it works, and then we'll do it). Prophetic Revolutionaries are the type of people who say, "I'm in it and I'll be the one that makes it work."

In verse 4, God tells Ezekiel what to prophesy. Revolutionaries don't just speak out any word. They speak the very words of God into a situation. In 1 Peter 4:11 it says,

> *"If anyone speaks, he should do so as one speaking the very words of God."*

The Word of God spoken into any situation has the amazing creative ability to make something happen (re-read the section about the power of the Word in Step #7, "Revolutionaries Understand Honour"). In this instance, Ezekiel prophesies the Word of God and something begins to happen immediately.

Many people like to hide away in their shell when difficult, dry times come against them. Audacious Revolutionaries rise with confidence and when it is dry, they start to prophesy and speak the very words of God.

The ability to prophesy in any given circumstance comes from spending time in the presence of God, with a Bible, a notebook and a pen. These moments of intimacy with God are as necessary as a soldier learning how to use his weapon before war breaks out. The Bible and the Spirit of God are the greatest weapons that a Revolutionary has in his arsenal. He sets out with diligence to learn the Scriptures and know the heart of God, so that when he is in the "valley of dry bones", he knows spiritually (probably instinctively) what he must do so he can see a "vast army" (verse 10) appear before him.

The Revolutionary doesn't view the "valley of dry bones" with fear and trepidation. The Revolutionary rises to the challenge, until he sees that "dead valley" come to life. The revolutionary sees dead people, but also sees what the future can hold for them when they finally say "Yes" to God.

Your Summary

Write your thoughts about this chapter here and what you need to do to in order to see dead people. How will this help you in evangelism?

"The Audacious Revolution" Summary

Nearly 500 years ago, Hugh Latimer said:

> "Be of good cheer, Master Ridley, and play the man, for we shall this day light such a candle in England as I trust by God's grace shall never be put out."

Thankfully, it never has. Since then Revolutionaries have carried the message of Jesus Christ into their world, whether they were schools, universities, colleges, workplaces, families or neighbourhoods. The facts about the "Audacious revolution" are simple:

- It's a power revolution
- It's a growing revolution
- It's an unstoppable revolution
- It's a Jesus revolution
- It's our revolution

The band POD rephrased Latimer's words and sang:

> This is my pledge and I'll take it to my death
> I'll lay my life down for you and die over again
> I'm not ashamed of the most high

Even if I die tonight, if I die tonight
This I pledge and I'll take it to my death
You can bet your life on my words and
everything I said
You can't take away my love for this sacrifice
Even if I die tonight, if I die tonight.[1]

Audacious Revolutionaries grow and develop in ten key areas:

1. They know what time it is /10
2. They are trouble causers /10
3. They know how to live amazing lives /10
4. They are the head not tail /10
5. They know they are called /10
6. They live fixed /10
7. They understand honour /10
8. They are enthusiastic /10
9. They have the lion spirit /10
10. They see dead people /10

To be a Revolutionary for the cause of Jesus Christ is more than just a decision you need to make – it is a recognition of your God-given birthright because of Jesus' accomplishment on the cross 2,000 years ago.

Give yourself a rating out of ten for each of the characteristics outlined above, making a conscious decision to develop all the key profiles in yourself.

Fill in the "Manifesto" as a statement of commitment to the cause of Jesus Christ and a determination to live as an "Audacious Revolutionary".

Notes

1. POD, lyrics from "The Messenjah" from the album *Satellite*, Atlantic Record Group, 2001.

The Revolutionary Manifesto

I, [name] ______________________________ commit myself to the cause of Jesus Christ while I have breath. I choose to live life as an "Audacious Revolutionary" determining always to:

- Know what time it is
- Cause trouble
- Live an amazing life
- Live as the head, not the tail
- Know I am called
- Live fixed
- Understand honour
- Be enthusiastic
- Live with the "lion spirit"
- See dead people

There is no greater name than the name of Jesus Christ and I choose to live to make His name great in my world!

Signed: ________________________ Date: __________

Contact Details

All inquiries regarding this publication and Glyn Barrett's speaking engagements should be made to,

The Hub
The Megacentre
Sheffield
S2 5BQ
Great Britain

Tel: +44 (0)114 272 5077
Email: info@liveaudacious.com

Information about Audacious, Youth Alive UK and Hope City Church can be found at:

www.liveaudacious.com
www.youthaliveuk.com
www.hopecity.co.uk